DAVE GELLY has been the jazz critic of *The Observer* for the last twelve years. He does regular TV and radio broadcasts on jazz and contemporary music, notably 'Night Owls', a weekly programme on BBC Radio 2. He has also written a biography of the tenor saxophone player, the late Lester Young.

DAVID SMITH, alias Weef, studied art in Leeds and moved to Edinburgh in 1977 where he contributed cartoons to many Scottish newspapers and magazines. He has had several exhibitions including one in the Traverse Theatre, Edinburgh. He is now a regular contributor to the *Sunday Express*, *Times Educational Supplement* and the *Scotsman Colour Magazine*.

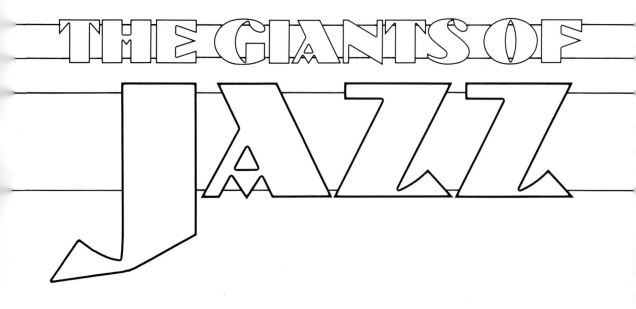

THE GIANTS OF JAZZ

DAVE GELLY · DRAWINGS BY WEEF

INTRODUCTION BY MILES KINGTON

AURUM PRESS

CONTENTS

INTRODUCTION

I wish I had had this book to help me when I first discovered jazz — an informed yet informal text with original drawings to bring each individual musician to life.

In the 1950s, when I was a jazz-hungry teenager, all the books about jazz were pretty serious affairs, full of record numbers, personnels for recording dates, charts of who-influenced-who, like cricket score-sheets. You got the impression, reading them, that afterwards you weren't meant to go out and enjoy the music; you were meant to take an A Level exam on the subject. If I wanted to, I could always find out who was playing third saxophone on any Benny Goodman date; what the books never told me was what it felt like to be playing for Benny Goodman, or even what it felt like to *be* Benny Goodman.

This book does. In fact, one of the funniest quotes in the book is attributed to Zoot Sims, who went on tour with Benny Goodman to Russia and was later asked what it was like touring in Russia. '*Every* gig with Benny is like playing in Russia,' he replied laconically. Now, the idea of an expert on jazz writing a book on jazz which contained funny quotes was not a common one when I was a lad and to be honest, it isn't so common today. Because jazz is an art and yet also part of showbiz, critics tend to play down the showbiz aspect and become even more serious than their classical counterparts.

Most critics not only write seriously, they also write boringly, almost as if the idea of bringing colour into your style is blasphemous. Nor for the most part do they play jazz, so that a vital element of first-hand experience is always missing; if you have never had a bad bass player plodding away behind you, it's hard to write about, and I can proudly boast that I have contributed a tiny fraction to this book as I once played bass in a band with Dave Gelly.

Gelly knows what jazz is all about. He knows what writing is all about. But he also knows what talking is all about, as the clearest impression that comes to me from this book is of an expert conversationalist chatting to you over a glass of something excellent and making a lot of things plain that usually remain cluttered. Read his entries on Nat Cole and Frank Sinatra, for example, where he explains that Cole was a fine jazz pianist who never sang like one, and Sinatra is no jazz musician yet can't help phrasing like one. At the end of these two brief accounts you'll know more about jazz than after reading many a complete book.

Writing a whole book about one person is probably easier than writing a swift portrait, and in setting out to sketch the identities of eighty giants of jazz, Gelly has had to rely on telling little details. He does it wonderfully well. Describing Basie's sparse piano style, for example, as 'the delicious agony of waiting for Basie to *do* something', or realizing that Sarah Vaughan really doesn't listen much to the words she's singing, with his reference to the way she always reduces *Send In The Clowns* to rubble. And when he says that Dave Brubeck was the leader of every band he played in, so he never had the self-indulgence knocked out of him, you feel that nothing more needs to be said.

Trying to work out Gelly's own likes and dislikes is a hard game to play, as apart from his frank confessions of distaste for Stan Kenton, Dave Brubeck and Buddy Rich, he seems to be fearfully fair-minded. But his remarks on Ray Brown and Bill Evans's bass players suggest fairly clearly why none of the trendy modern bass players like Stanley Clarke or Ron Carter get their own entry, and lovers of Arts Council jazz will look in vain for pieces on Cecil Taylor, Keith Jarrett or Chick Corea. Nor do I remember any mention of Weather Report, which suits me fine but may upset a few.

I would also be disposed to query a few of his statements, such as his theory that Erroll Garner had no imitators. I would bet that every country in the world has boasted a native who, at one time or another, thought he was a reincarnation of Garner – I remember seeing a French pianist called Ralph Schecroun who not only played just like Garner but also insisted on sitting on a phone directory, just like his hero.

And when he says that it is very rare to find a jazz musician whose playing is utterly unlike his everyday self, I know what he means, and yet Pete King, the manager of Ronnie Scott's Club, once put a theory to me that stated the exact opposite. The fiery, roaring tenor players, he said, are usually the mildest of men off the stand; it's the ones with the silky suave styles who turn out to be the trouble-makers and all-round evil characters.

'Who's the silkiest, suavest tenor player you can think of?' he said.

I named him. Pete King nodded, satisfied.

'He was the worst bastard we ever had at the club. Absolutely impossible.'

Libel laws prevent me from naming him, but he is featured in this book . . . And now I find that I have started talking back to Dave Gelly's book, which is exactly the effect that such a book should have. It tells you a lot of things, even if you think you know it all, but it never talks down to you, just makes you want to respond.

MILES KINGTON

PREFACE

The first artist depicted here, King Oliver, was born in 1885. Almost all the others were born in the subsequent sixty years, the period between the invention of sound recording and the arrival of modern mass communications.

Jazz was born at roughly the same time as the phonograph and therefore was the first form of local popular music to be able to travel beyond its home territory. Hitherto, only written music had this freedom, and the European classical tradition spread as a result. But most of the world's music is not written down. It exists only in performance; it is player's music, not composer's music. Before someone invented the means of recording sound, entire musical cultures must have risen and declined, leaving no trace.

On the other hand, recording and radio have, in turn, strangled the distinctive musical cultures of the United States and other Western countries in recent times. Whereas, half a century ago, one could have found dozens of regional styles, today there are only radio play-lists. Jazz developed as luxuriantly as it did because it turned up at the right moment.

Naturally, once musicians were able to speak with their own voices, the voices themselves became a vital part of what was said. The characters in this book are all important voices, immediately recognizable and wonderfully varied. The majority, of course, are black Americans, but jazz stopped being a purely ethnic music very early in its life. First it became an all-American musical language, and then spread through most of the world. Other nations speak it with their own accents – there is even a distinctive Russian jazz accent – and it has followers everywhere. In Europe during World War Two jazz was banned by the Nazis as being the product of degenerate races, yet even German record companies continued to issue occasional jazz records, and bands in the occupied countries carried on playing, sometimes changing tune titles for purposes of discretion; *St Louis Blues*, for instance, became *La Tristesse de Saint Louis*.

Jazz itself has never been the most popular form, but it has been present in solution, so to speak, in almost all popular music since the end of World War One. The most far-reaching effect of jazz on the general public has been to change utterly the idea of what constitutes an acceptable musical sound. Even in the late thirties, for instance, most British people would agree that the only 'good singing voice' was a voice trained in the European tradition, like Richard Tauber's or John McCormack's. Nowadays a 'good voice' is just as likely to belong to George Benson or Ray Charles.

Jazz writers are very keen on movements, schools and lines of influence. This is fair enough, since the history of jazz is the story of an oral tradition – of things handed down. But this book is a collection of individual portraits, with only passing reference to the general history. There are many scholarly works which do the job far better than we could manage here.

A good cartoon not only picks out and exaggerates certain physical features, it also manages to convey the essence of the subject's personality. It is strange that so few cartoonists have, until now, concentrated on jazz musicians, because the music does exactly the same thing. It is very rare to find a jazz musician whose music is utterly unlike his everyday self. Clifford Brown, for example, was a human sunbeam who radiated goodwill and high spirits. Listen to his ebullient playing, and then glance at Weef's cherubic cartoon. The one echoes the other to perfection.

As for the text, I have tried to give some idea of what is special about each of the artists included, and roughly where each one fits into the jazz picture. It would be idle to pretend that these are completely neutral views; admirers of, say, Dave Brubeck and Stan Kenton are bound to disagree with my remarks, but neutrality in matters of taste is not a virtue. At least I am as sure as I can reasonably be about facts; if the odd factual error has crept in, then it is entirely my fault, although I have tried to double-check such things as dates.

I cannot claim any credit for the conception of the book. The original idea came from Weef (David Smith) and he worked on the book with the late Derek Jewell, who was for many years jazz and popular music critic of the *Sunday Times* and author of several respected books in the field. Sadly, Derek died during the final planning stages, before he had written more than a few entries. With some minor emendations I have stuck to his original plan – not out of respect, but because it was so well devised.

Finally, I would like to thank *The Observer* for permission to include a few brief passages from pieces which I have contributed to the newspaper in recent years.

DAVE GELLY

King Oliver

b. 11 May 1885

d. 10 April 1938

Louis Armstrong, who scarcely knew his own father, always referred to Joe 'King' Oliver as 'Papa Joe', and it is as a beaming, avuncular, stern-but-kindly figure that Oliver has passed into history.

The first great creation-myth of jazz is, in fact, the story of King Oliver. Born in 1885, he rose as a young man to the position of top cornet player in New Orleans (hence the title 'King') during that now almost mythical time before the First World War, when the city was a wide-open town, with everything tolerated, and usually done to a musical accompaniment.

When the US Navy decided, in 1917, that enough was far more than enough, and closed down 'Storeyville' and other New Orleans red-light districts, Oliver took his music north. He settled finally in Chicago, leading a band almost exclusively composed of musicians from his native city and, once established, sent for his protegé Armstrong. His fondness for the young man was tempered by practicality: 'So long as he's with me he can't hurt me,' he observed.

The records made during 1923 by King Oliver's Creole Jazz Band are the first jazz classics. They were recorded by the only method then available, the acoustic system, which involved the musicians playing into a large horn. The results are surprisingly good for such crude apparatus, but they do require a bit of perseverance to recreate mentally the original sound. Once you do this, however, you realize what a sensational band Oliver had – and how much better it was than anything else then in existence. There is a sweeping, unhesitating confidence about it, enormous intricacy and, beneath it all, that rolling New Orleans beat which marks out, even today, musicians raised in that city.

The Creole Jazz Band played at the Lincoln Gardens, a nightclub which found itself doubling as a music academy when players, both black and white, came from all over Chicago and beyond to listen and take notes before going away to practise. In particular, they were utterly baffled by the famous Oliver–Armstrong duet breaks. The rhythm section would stop and the two cornets would improvise a perfectly harmonized two-bar phrase without any apparent preparation. Years later Armstrong confided that Oliver would whisper a phrase in his ear when no-one was looking, and they would have it ready. But even so it's a stupendous feat of musicianship.

When the Creole Jazz Band broke up, and Armstrong went on to greater glories, Oliver formed a bigger band, the Dixie Syncopators, which included a saxophone section. It was still a splendid band, but couldn't possibly live up to its predecessor. Gradually Oliver's fortunes declined. Fashion was moving away from his style of music, thanks partly to Louis Armstrong and his virtuoso star performances. To make matters worse, Oliver developed a gum disease which at first made playing the cornet painful, and finally impossible.

He died in 1938 in Atlanta, Georgia, employed as the sweeper-up in a third-rate pool hall.

JELLY ROLL MORTON

b. 20 October 1890

d. 10 July 1941

New Orleans coloured creoles ('les gens de couleur libres') were very special people, a nation within a nation. They were of mixed race, and from their forebears had inherited French sophistication, Spanish pride, African grace. They led an elegant life in nineteenth century New Orleans, more Mediterranean than American in flavour, and cultivated the arts keenly and with flair. Then, in the 1880s, a law was enacted in the State of Louisiana declaring that all persons with any 'coloured blood' were now to be classified as 'negroes'. Being lumped with illiterate ex-slaves and excluded from the polite world was a tremendous blow to creole pride and paranoia was widespread when Jelly Roll Morton (born Ferdinand LaMothe, or LaMenthe, or possibly Lemott) arrived in 1890. It is not surprising that he grew up a suspicious, quarrelsome, greedy, self-pitying man. He also grew up to become a blindingly good pianist, a bandleader of genius and the first true jazz composer. That should have been enough, but he also claimed that he had 'invented' jazz and that everyone was stealing it from him. He wasted time, money and friendships in campaigns to prove this ludicrous claim, and ended up broke as a result.

Morton's stature as a composer rests mainly on two series of recordings, the piano solos which he made for the Gennett label of Richmond, Indiana in 1923–4 and the work of his band Jelly Roll Morton's Red Hot Peppers, recorded for Victor between 1926 and 1929. His style was much more varied than ragtime, with all kinds of expressive effects in the extreme treble and bass, and much play made with dynamics.

Equally important was the influence of the music and rhythms of the Spanish Carib-bean. In all of Morton's work you can hear the characteristic syncopated Habanera patterns sliding in underneath.

In transferring all this to a small band, Morton established a working method which has, more or less, been followed by the best jazz composers ever since. He would sketch out introduction, order of solos, bridge passages and coda, then play through the piece a few times, letting the other musicians improvise their own solos and changing things around to fit, until he ended up with a kind of shaped improvisation, so natural-sounding that you only notice the cunning of the thing when you stop to analyze it. Perfect examples of this method in operation are the Red Hot Peppers' *Black Bottom Stomp, The Chant* and *Grandpa's Spells* – all from 1926.

Jelly Roll Morton was a rich and successful bandleader during the twenties. The Peppers had the pick of private functions, society balls and rich people's parties.

But, as with King Oliver, Morton fell from public favour in the thirties. His health declined, and he even had to sell his prized symbol of success, the diamond set between his front teeth.

However, towards the end, while he was vainly trying to run a club in Washington DC, in 1938, the folklorist Alan Lomax got him to record his memoirs for the Library of Congress archives. As the only really full first-hand account of the early days of jazz in New Orleans, these are almost as valuable as the works of his great period.

JAMES P. JOHNSON

b. 1 February 1894
d. 17 November 1955

The style known as 'stride piano' was, broadly speaking, the offspring of a marriage between ragtime and the blues: city and country, gentility and earthiness, constraint and drive. James P. Johnson was its first great master (although closely pursued by Eubie Blake, Willie 'The Lion' Smith and others) and teacher of the finest of them all, Thomas 'Fats' Waller.

In stride piano the form of ragtime is retained, with its multiple themes and modulations, but there is a new impetus behind it. The melody is no longer tied squarely to the pulse but seems to be pulling against it, creating little eddies and cross-currents. The whole thing hangs on the beat created by the left hand, alternating a single bass note with a chord voiced towards the middle of the keyboard. This is the 'stride' which gives its name to the style.

The classic stride pianists, like Johnson, were not improvisors; their pieces were far too complicated to be made up on the spur of the moment, but they had a headlong verve to them which was far more exciting than the formal patterns of ragtime. Johnson's most famous composition *Carolina Shout* is a perfect example of the style. It was always regarded as the test piece by which pianists were judged; if they could play the *Shout*, they were in business.

Stride piano flourished in the crowded Harlem of the decade following World War One, where innumerable pianists could be found emulating Johnson and co while playing at 'rent parties' and other semi-legal, semi-private functions.

Also to be heard at such gatherings were the blues singers of the period, mainly women, of whom Bessie Smith was the greatest. James P. Johnson can be heard accompanying her on several of her most celebrated records, including *Backwater Blues* and *Any Woman's Blues*.

SMITH
Bessie

b. 15 April 1895

d. 26 September 1937

The short film *St Louis Blues*, made in 1929 and starring Bessie Smith, is no work of art, but it does present in distilled form what would nowadays be called the 'image' of the female blues artists of the time, of whom Bessie was the greatest. The story depicts her as a wronged and exploited woman. Her man, a flashy and unappetizing character, rejects her and beats her up, before leaving with a young girl. He returns briefly, but only to steal her money.

Bessie is left drinking whisky and singing the blues, and this is one of the two basic narratives of her songs. The other tells the opposite tale, of the sexually voracious woman discarding a worn-out lover: 'You've been a good ole wagon, but now you done broke down.' In fact, Bessie was closer to the second than the first of these stereotypes, although she did drink a huge amount.

The blues and jazz live in a symbiotic relationship, but the two are actually separate and there are almost as many styles of blues as there are of jazz. The 'classic' blues of Bessie Smith grew out of black vaudeville and the touring tent-shows of the early years of this century.

In the mid-twenties Bessie Smith was earning around 2,000 dollars a week, an enormous sum in those days. She was idolized by black audiences and by a sizeable coterie of whites, to whom negritude symbolized emotional honesty and sexual freedom. The writer and avant-garde figure Carl Van Vechten worshipped Bessie and made a series of photographic studies of her in various moods.

Nevertheless, Bessie Smith was far more than a fashionable popular figure. A big, statuesque woman, she had all the presence of a great tragic actress; even in a tatty vehicle like *St Louis Blues* this is evident. Her singing voice was deep and passionate, with a dark, accusing quality to it, and her phrasing was grave and stately. No matter how worldly or lewd the lyrics, there was nothing skittish about Bessie.

Her recording career lasted from 1923 to 1933; all her recorded work was for the Columbia label and it has all been reissued since her death, most notably in five double albums produced in the 1970s. Although her voice lost some of its grandeur towards the end, there is very little change in her approach over the course of the decade, and some of her performances are almost unbearable in their power: *Nobody Knows You When You're Down and Out, Empty Bed Blues, Young Woman's Blues*, and the sublime duets with the young Louis Armstrong in *Cold In Hand Blues, Reckless Blues* and *St Louis Blues*.

The period of classic blues represented by Bessie Smith's records seems now like a remote age; it had vanished entirely by the early thirties. Popular sensibility changed so suddenly and so completely at the turn of the decade that Bessie's style, along with those of Oliver and Morton, took on an instant patina of age, a sepia-tinted distance. And yet she lived on into the swing era – until 1937, in fact.

Her end was more lurid than anything in the most doom-laden blues song. Travelling to an engagement in Mississippi, she was fatally injured in a road accident near Clarksdale. The legend grew up that she had bled to death after being refused admission to a white hospital. This was later disproved, but the story provided the theme of Edward Albee's play *The Death of Bessie Smith*, and legends usually prove more durable than fact.

SIDNEY BECHET

| b. 14 May 1897 |
| d. 14 May 1959 |

Sidney Bechet's life was exactly like his playing: wilful, truculent and domineering, but throbbing with passion and vitality. He was a New Orleans creole, like Morton, born right in the middle of that remarkable generation which stretches from Oliver to Armstrong, yet he was never really part of the great flowering of New Orleans music in Chicago and New York during the twenties. He was one of nature's wanderers, and usually somewhere else when the classic records were being made.

His travels took him across the United States and Europe – to Britain, France, Germany and Russia. And he went as a featured artist, a virtuoso soloist with big musical productions, first with Will Marion Cook's Southern Syncopated Orchestra and later with a show called the Revue Negre. This explains, at least partly, his forceful and self-sufficient style of playing. He never went through the kind of apprenticeship that Armstrong and the others had, no playing in a succession of bands and working his way up. He began as a teenage prodigy and always expected to be the centre of attention. And he was.

Few places he visited had ever heard any jazz at all so Bechet, with his broad tone and bold, sweeping phrases on the clarinet, and later soprano saxophone, came as a revelation. But his headlong approach to life got him into quite a lot of trouble too. He was jailed in England and then deported because of a fight involving a prostitute, and in France he served almost a year behind bars.

He also had a stormy love affair with Bessie Smith at around this time. When Bechet did descend on the jazz centres of America he caused a mighty stir. The 1924 record of *Cake Walking Babies* by the Red Onion Jazz Babies includes both him and Armstrong. Each is obviously working flat-out to eclipse the other and the result, after a series of stupendous solo breaks, is a dead heat.

And so he went on through the 1930s making a few brilliant records (the ones by his New Orleans Feetwarmers are particularly fine) and taking off at a moment's notice. He didn't build a career like Armstrong's; at one point Bechet even gave up music in disgust and opened a tailor's shop. He might well have ended up as the kind of legendary figure who is more legend than anything else – a few brilliant records and a vast fund of anecdotes passed down the generations. But this didn't happen, because history had plans for him.

New Orleans-style jazz had suddenly fallen out of fashion at the end of the twenties. By the late thirties a 'revival' had begun, not with the public at large but with a growing band of enthusiasts. Bechet found himself almost as a figurehead. Oliver and Morton died too young to benefit from the revival, and Armstrong had become a big star and wasn't interested. Bechet, who looked older than his years anyway, took on the part of Grand Old Man with aplomb.

In 1949 he appeared at the first Paris Jazz Fair, and here began his final elevation – this time to the status of national hero. He moved to France and married a Frenchwoman. His playing took on a distinctly Gallic character and his records sold literally in millions, rivalling even those of Edith Piaf in popularity.

When he died in 1959 (on his 62nd birthday) France practically went into mourning. A statue of Sidney Bechet was erected near his home at Antibes, in a square which they named after him. The hoodlum and jailbird of former years could have been a different man.

DUKE ELLINGTON

b. 29 April 1899

d. 24 May 1974

Musical entertainment for tourists – 'the locals letting themselves go with their spirited music and dancing' type of thing – is inevitably hideous. Grinning flamenco dancers, Neapolitan tenors bawling 'Santa Lucia' through microphones, chirpy stage cockneys doing the Lambeth Walk, they're all cruel mockeries, and demeaning to all concerned. With this in mind, consider the Cotton Club, Harlem, in 1927: a white nightclub in a black ghetto, featuring a stage show full of jungles, prancing natives, cooking pots, tropical thunderstorms and black girls with very little on – especially the latter. Entrusted with producing suitable music to accompany this farrago was an urbane young pianist of good family from Washington DC, Edward Kennedy Ellington, known as Duke, the only person in history to have turned tourist art into real art. The amazing thing about it is that throughout almost half a century, from *Jungle Nights in Harlem* to the *Third Sacred Concert*, it's clearly the same man, the same mind and many of the same orchestral techniques.

The whole world knows that Duke Ellington is the greatest jazz composer, but it is now becoming accepted that he is one of the great composers of any kind in this century. However you define jazz (and it's a pretty self-defeating exercise), Ellington consistently went beyond it. His large-scale works, such as *Black Brown and Beige* and *Such Sweet Thunder*, the numerous concert suites and the oratorios called Sacred Concerts would not fit many people's definitions, but they could not have been written by

anyone else, which is to say anyone but the man who also composed *Ko Ko, Harlem Airshaft, Cottontail* and the rest. His view of the matter seems to have been that he would make whatever music he liked, and it was up to other people to make fools of themselves by trying to fit it into their absurd categories.

He was able to take this confident stance because, in the first place, he could afford to. Along with everything else, Ellington is one of the great American songwriters and the income from numbers like *Sophisticated Lady, Don't Get Around Much Any More* and *Solitude* made him wealthy and independent. It also enabled him to keep his orchestra in being through the tough years, when even Basie was forced to disband. 'If I write something today, I want to *hear* it today,' he said. And, of course, only his band could play his work, because the parts were written for particular players.

But money only partly explains his confidence. More fundamental was the fact that he came from a secure, affectionate, reasonably well-off family, had always been popular and a social success, and always did quite well in whatever he decided to undertake. In short, he was living confirmation of the idea that art-for-art's-sake is a commodity reserved solely for the middle classes.

Before taking up music seriously, Duke had been intending to study art, and was indeed offered an NAACP scholarship to go to art school. It is hardly surprising, then, that his approach to music should be impressionistic and much concerned with the mixing of colours and textures in orchestration. There is not a single Ellington recording in which some beguiling combination of instruments fails to occur, or one of the well known voices in the Ellington reper-

tory company does not pop out at an unexpected moment. The effect of the band in person was simply shattering. It was as though an enormous, many-tongued human voice was shouting at you. The combination of Duke's thick-textured writing, the broad tones of the saxophone section, the barking power of the brass, and a sort of loose-jointed flexibility in the way they played together, made it an experience no-one could forget.

There is simply so much Ellington music on record that it's not possible to make a 'best of' selection, although some have tried. By common consent the orchestra reached its highest peak in the period from 1940 to 1942, when it contained a particularly rich collection of musicians, including the bass player Jimmy Blanton. Over his light, skipping line the band swung more than ever, and Duke produced some of his most distinguished work for it – *Concerto For Cootie, Harlem Airshaft, Sepia Panorama, Jack The Bear* – all beautifully organized miniatures, timed to fit exactly into the three-minute length of the ten-inch 78rpm record. By contrast, his suite of Shakespearean sketches, *Such Sweet Thunder*, is much more than just a collection of short pieces, having a distinct atmosphere which permeates the whole work. It also contains some of the boldest orchestration in all Ellington's output, but every now and then you catch a fleeting echo of the old Cotton Club growl, a sudden flare of sound that recalls the nightclub jungle.

THE ELLINGTONIANS

Ellington composed not for instruments but for people. That's what made his music so vibrantly human. Here are just a few of the musicians whose voices were part of his voice, individuals who remained themselves, even though they will forever be thought of as Ellingtonians.

Joe 'Tricky Sam' Nanton

b. 1 February 1904
d. 20 July 1946

Tricky Sam was not a virtuoso. In any other context his playing would still have been instantly identifiable, but only as a minor, slightly eccentric source of exotic effects. In Ellington's band, however, Nanton achieved greatness and a unique eloquence. He came closer than any other jazz player to the literal sound of the human voice. By manipulating the rubber plunger mute he made the trombone speak – crying, shouting, pleading, declaiming. No-one ever approached his aptitude for speaking through an instrument, and few ever tried. Others played faster, higher and with more polish – but Tricky Sam spoke with his own authentic voice.

Johnny Hodges

b. 25 July 1907

d. 11 May 1970

Ellington's orchestral scores are extraordinary documents. Scrawled amidst the conventional notation one finds various hieroglyphics and occasional words. Very often a phrase, even a single note, will be ringed in pencil and marked with the name of a particular player. One word appears often: 'Rabbit'. This was the band's nickname for alto saxophonist Johnny Hodges. His silky, slippery tones were essential to many of Duke's compositions, and at certain points nothing else would do.

Rabbit, easing up to a note, could set the tone of a whole piece, which is why Duke made sure he played that particular note. Hodges would have been a great soloist even without Ellington, and he proved it by going out on his own several times, but he is heard at his very best when leading the saxophone section or floating over the orchestra in full-throated song.

Ben Webster

b. 27 March 1909

d. 20 September 1973

Tough and tender, gruff and melting, Ben Webster's tenor saxophone was one of the few Ellingtonian voices to go on to an independent existence beyond the orchestra. *Just A'Sittin' And A'Rockin'* and *Cotton-tail* were his most celebrated features with the band, the one silky and insinuating, the other urgent and driving. But Ben went on to develop a breathy, blowsy style of playing ballads which had only been hinted at in his Ellingtonian days. Towards the end of his life (he died in 1973) he moved to Europe, where he was lionized by jazz fans. In his later work the breath gradually invades the notes, until every phrase ends with a vibrating column of air, slowly fading into silence, like the Cheshire Cat's grin.

Harry Carney

b. 1 April 1910
d. 8 October 1974

The longest-serving member of the orchestra, Harry Carney was with Duke for 47 years – almost from first to last. He was his friend and confidant, and the rock upon which the Ellingtonian sound was built. Carney's tone on baritone saxophone was enormous, ripe and broad and singing. Of all the colours in Duke's palette, his was the most indispensable. It is impossible to imagine Ellington's music without Harry Carney. When Duke died, Harry retired. There was nothing else to do, and he contemptuously dismissed an offer to join a 'memories of Duke' band. Although he had always enjoyed robust good health, he died only five months after Duke.

Cootie Williams

b. 24 July 1910

d. 15 September 1985

Ferocious – that's the only word to describe Cootie's trumpet. Growling and snarling, he prowled through the orchestral jungle like a dangerous beast. He even *looked* terrifying, scowling and tensing himself before unleashing one of his livid solos. And yet he was a gentle person, quiet and trusting. When he left Ellington in 1940, Duke said, 'If you ever feel like coming back, the place is yours.' Twenty-two years later Cootie reclaimed his place and carried on exactly as before.

One of Ellington's greatest compositions was *Concerto For Cootie*, written around him rather than for him.

LOUIS ARMSTRONG

b. 4 July 1900

d. 6 July 1971

If a certain judge had taken the view that boys will be boys, and let him off with a caution, Louis Armstrong might never have become a trumpet player. In that event, jazz would probably not exist now in its present form and the whole history of Western music would therefore have taken a different course. But the judge, surveying the small, black, ragged figure before him, decided that the offence of discharging a firearm in the public street – even on New Year's Eve – merited a custodial sentence. Very likely he also considered the boy would be better looked after in the New Orleans Waifs' Home than in the bosom of his own family – and he was right. And so the young Armstrong (age uncertain, because his date of birth is uncertain) was led away into genial captivity. They put him in the choir and he learned his parts quickly; they gave him a tambourine to shake and a drum to bang, both of which he managed without difficulty. Then they let him blow a bugle, then an alto horn, and then a cornet. Soon he was leading the band.

When they let him out, Louis got a job delivering coal during the day and playing casual engagements in dance halls at night. Soon he was spotted by the top cornettist of the day, Joe 'King' Oliver, who treated him as his protegé. When Oliver left town to try his luck in Chicago he passed his job on to Louis. By the age of about 18 Louis Armstrong was the man to watch in New Orleans. Then, in 1922, Oliver sent for him to join his Creole Jazz Band in Chicago, and it was with King Oliver that Armstrong played his first solo chorus on record, in a version of *Chimes Blues*. Even at this age it was obvious that Louis was different from any jazz musician who had come before him. His tone was broad, warm and filled with a kind of smiling humanity, his technique was astounding and his range unheard of – but the thing which really marked him out was his stupendous inventiveness and the sheer elegance of his improvised line.

Oliver could not hold him for long. Even though Louis felt deep ties of loyalty, he had to leave. Anyway, he had married Oliver's pianist, Lil Hardin, and she had enough

ambition for both of them. From the moment of leaving Oliver, Louis was never again to be a mere member of a band; he was either a featured soloist or a bandleader in his own right, and it is in this role that he became the determining influence on the entire course of jazz. He made it into an improvising soloist's art, focused what had hitherto been a collection of vague notions about 'hot music' on to one central element – the fluid line deployed over a regular beat and moving harmonies.

Because Louis went on to become a world-famous entertainer and, ultimately, a show-business institution, because he gradually turned into lovable old Satchmo, because he was a showman, a scene-stealer – because, in short, he is such a vast, uncontainable *fact* in the popular art of the century – this achievement is often cited almost in passing, if not ignored altogether, but it is immensely important.

Louis Armstrong didn't issue written instructions about the way jazz was to proceed: he simply played, and the result was so overwhelming that no-one could help falling into line behind him. There were plenty of show-off trumpet players around at the time, but Louis wasn't showing off. He was constructing musical statements that were both fluid and massive, passionate and logical, juxtaposing long, arching melodies and short, clipped phrases so that they formed a perfect balance. *Potato Head Blues, West End Blues, Weatherbird* and dozens more from his first decade as a soloist are marvels not just of playing but of mental agility and imaginative power. Armstrong's biographer, James Lincoln Collier, speculated about the mind that could organize material with such effortless mastery. Had Louis been born into the white professional middle classes, Collier mused, might he have become not a musician but an architect or a playwright?

But would he also have been born without the killer instinct which is part of the make-up of all successful entertainers? Louis had that in the same undiluted quantities as Frank Sinatra or Judy Garland had it. He would not share applause with anyone on equal terms. On his deathbed he insisted on getting up to give one more show. He loved the applause, he needed the adulation; he could not contemplate life without them. His great decade (from about 1925 to 1935) was the period when he was getting established. Once the movie parts and radio shows and national tours began rolling in he was happy to do what was needed in order to keep them coming. There was nothing cynical in this. As Collier has also pointed out, the very idea of the artist having a special kind of sensibility was foreign to him. He never did quite understand what it was that all those intellectual writers were making a fuss about in his old records.

BiX BEIDERBECKE

b. 10 March 1903
d. 6 August 1931

Bix Beiderbecke was the first white jazz musician of undoubted greatness. Without exception, his contemporaries were awed by his talent, and captivated by the unique tone which he produced from the cornet. One jazz writer likened his cornet solos to 'shooting bullets at a bell'.

The Beiderbecke style is lithe and glancing with elegant twists and turns. This, ever since, has been the distinguishing mark of white jazz.

Unlike Louis, his near contemporary, Bix had behind him not the heritage of the blues, but the European musical tradition brought to America by his German ancestors. His unique contribution to jazz history, apart from his own genius, was to establish a style in which European notions of pitch and tone fitted happily into the Afro-American idiom. From Bix Beiderbecke to Benny Goodman to Stan Getz, the line can be followed quite clearly.

For more than half a century Bix Beiderbecke has been the subject of enthusiastic myth-making. Consider the outline of his life-story: respectable mid-West background, seduced by outlandish noises coming from the gramophone, self-taught, meteoric rise, early death from drink. Add to this the fact that he lived and worked in Prohibition America and the romantic picture is complete.

While it is certainly true that Bix became an alcoholic and died young as a result, in other respects he was much more the loyal child of his background than a rebel. He was inordinately proud of being a member of Paul Whiteman's 'symphonic jazz' orchestra and the ponderous respectability which it represented, and proud of a series of piano pieces which he composed, in the 'light classical' manner of the day – *In A Mist, Candlelight* etc.

But Bix's great work really appears in the cornet solos – bright, bubbling, innocent, optimistic – which he recorded in less than ten years of fully active musical life.

At 20, he recorded with the Wolverines, an enthusiastic but unremarkable young band. Later he joined the dance band of Gene Goldkette and, finally, the Whiteman orchestra. It was with small groups drawn mainly from their ranks that he recorded his finest work. The celebrated *Singin' The Blues* became almost a test-piece for would-be cornet players, while *Wringin' And Twistin', Humpty Dumpty, Since My Best Girl Turned Me Down* and many others reveal why Bix was one of the most imitated musicians of his generation.

Jimmy Rushing

b. 26 August 1903

d. 8 June 1972

Mr Five-By-Five was Jimmy Rushing's nickname – five feet tall and five feet wide – but the general effect was spherical rather than rectangular. From this 20-stone frame issued a curiously high-pitched voice, a voice to carry over a dance floor crowded with revellers in the days when a microphone could not be relied upon, even if there was one.

Rushing was the vocalist with Count Basie's miraculous first band, alongside Lester Young, Buck Clayton, Dickie Wells and other young masters of the art. Although he was often referred to as a 'blues shouter', more than half his recordings with Basie (between 1936 and 1948) consist of current pop songs and standards, and these display his superb talent for making a tune swing by means of simple phrasing and forceful delivery. His slow blues are often tinged with a kind of resigned melancholy, rather than passion, and his sometimes bawdy up-tempo blues sound almost innocent in their relish.

Despite his girth he never cut a clownish figure, although there is a priceless little movie, a five-minute short made in the mid-forties, in which he plays the part of a rejected suitor who sings his way back into the young lady's affections while navigating with great care around the flimsy prop-furniture.

After leaving Basie he enjoyed a busy and fulfilling career for almost a quarter of a century, first as a bandleader at the Savoy Ballroom in Harlem, and then as a solo artist, travelling the world. He never grew out of his youthful delight in music and the company of musicians. I can recall several evenings at London jazz clubs which turned into late-night jam sessions because Jimmy Rushing felt like making a night of it.

FATS WALLER

b. 21 May 1904
d. 15 December 1943

Fats was blessed with enormous musical gifts, an endless facility for making up tunes and a fun-loving nature which captivated everyone he met. He was also cursed with chronic alcoholism and a sense of guilt at not having lived up to his God-fearing parents' expectations.

He started teaching himself the piano at the age of six and by his mid-teens was a professional, playing the organ in a Harlem cinema. At this time he was taken on as a kind of apprentice by the great James P. Johnson, and from him learned the art of stride piano. Fats was soon a successful pianist, much in demand at Harlem parties, accompanying vaudeville acts and occasionally working as a session pianist in radio and recording studios. In 1927 he and Johnson composed the music for the popular review *Keep Shufflin'*, and two years later he wrote the score for the Broadway hit *Hot Chocolates*.

To a more careful man this would have set the pattern for a prosperous career, but Fats would dash off something, sell it outright and head for a night on the town. With lyricist Andy Razaf he composed some of the best known songs in the American repertoire: *Ain't Misbehavin'*, *Honeysuckle Rose*, *Keepin' Out Of Mischief Now*. He is believed to have written at least 300 published pieces, although many more may have been sold and subsequently claimed by others.

His solo piano pieces, such as *Alligator Crawl*, *Clothes Line Ballet* and *Viper's Drag*, represent the pinnacle of the Harlem stride idiom. Looser and more wayward than Johnson's, they are nevertheless fully composed works but with the carefree, improvised quality of true jazz.

It was in the final decade of his life, from 1934, that the Fats Waller that everyone knows was born – the derby-hatted mountain of jollity, the Harmful Little Armful. It began at a party given by George Gershwin, who revered the stride pianists and would sit listening to them by the hour. At one such gathering, with Fats in fine form, a record company executive heard him and arranged a contract with Victor records. The idea was for Fats to do what he did at parties – sing and play and radiate good humour – in the company of a small band. They called the group 'Fats Waller and his Rhythm', and the format made him into an international star.

In just over nine years the Rhythm produced enough three-minute numbers to fill 30 modern twelve-inch albums, and that accounts only for the official Victor sessions. The material varied from excellent to dire, but Fats didn't seem to mind. If the song was not much good he would send it up, lapsing into gargling operatic parody.

The Rhythm could record up to ten tunes in a single session. The arrangements were the simplest possible, usually just outline routines with an all-in burst of 16 bars or so at the end. This is probably why they still sound so fresh today, when full-dress arrangements of the period have faded into insipidity and dullness.

Fats was still on his way up at the time of his death. His short appearance in the film *Stormy Weather*, starring Lena Horne, effectively stole the show and he was clearly on course for stardom of at least Louis Armstrong dimensions. But drink, irregular hours and overwork finally did for him. He was 39 when he died suddenly, aboard the 'Santa Fe Chief' in a howling blizzard, just outside Kansas City.

COUNT

b. 21 August 1904

d. 26 April 1984

You never saw a man happy in his work until you saw Bill Basie at the piano beside his band. He would sit motionless, except for his eyes, watching the beautiful, exact machine he had created ticking over smoothly, and then, 'bink, bink – bink!' – three tiny icicles would drop with devilish precision into the middle of it all, accompanied by the merest flicker of an eyebrow. It never failed.

When he died, just before his eightieth birthday, Basie had been leading his band for almost half a century. It began in 1935 at the Reno Club in Kansas City, a mere nine-piece outfit playing for dancing and a floorshow. This was the sound that critic and record producer John Hammond heard by accident on his car radio late one night in a Chicago parking lot. Thanks to Hammond's efforts, Basie brought the band, now enlarged to fourteen members, to New York and almost instant acclaim.

In many ways it was the best he ever had, with soloists such as the trumpeter Buck Clayton, trombonist Dickie Wells and, finest of all, the tenor saxophonist Lester Young. Listening today to records by that first Count Basie Orchestra one needs to make no adjustment of historical perspective to appreciate its greatness. The bursting energy of the ensemble, the poise and resourcefulness of the soloists, the matchless spring of the rhythm section – all unite to create an effortless, authoritative flow which denies the passing years. Only Ellington, in his totally different way, is worthy of comparison.

As time passed, Basie's piano playing became ever more sparse. When he started out he employed the big,

BASIE

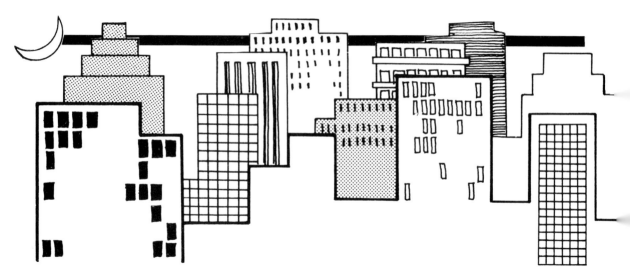

fully-voiced stride style, as befitted a pupil of Fats Waller, but gradually this was polished down almost to nothing. As the layers of rhetoric fell away, he became ever more eloquent, his timing a source of wonder and despair to other pianists. The delicious agony of waiting for Basie to *do* something was always rewarded when he finally did it.

Leading a band isn't easy, and most bandleaders are heartily disliked by the musicians they employ, but you can comb the jazz books and I guarantee you will not find an unaffectionate word about Basie. He was so modest that he seemed like the last man for the job. His secret was that he was always more a musician than a leader. For years he travelled in the band bus, playing poker through the night and swapping stories, instead of acting like the star of the show. In later years the going was fairly comfortable, but for a black band in the thirties and forties life on the road was hard and undignified. The musicians never forgot that Basie chose to share it with them.

As the personnel of the orchestra changed, its sound changed too. By the fifties it had developed into a massive, flexible, swinging machine. This was when it acquired the status of an international institution, and when British audiences first had the chance to experience it in person. I shall never forget the excitement of those first Basie tours, the curtain opening on the sixteen uniformed figures casually launching into *The Kid From Red Bank*, and the man himself cutting off the number with a gentle, dismissive wave of his left hand. In his uninsistent way he summed up the spirit of jazz in that one gesture.

COLEMAN HAWKINS

b. 21 November 1904
d. 19 May 1969

It is often said that Coleman Hawkins invented the saxophone as a jazz instrument, and there is more than a grain of truth in the observation. The saxophone was invented in the 1840s by the Belgian instrument maker Adolphe Sax, as a sort of optional extra for military bands. It is a hybrid, a cross between brass and woodwind, with a clarinet-type mouthpiece and reed and a brass body. During the early years of this century, when public dancing became all the rage, the saxophone was brought indoors as part of the dance orchestra. Its braying, sugary tones were much louder than half a dozen violins, and thus easier to hear over the sounds of revelry and shuffling feet. But it was not a pretty noise. The general effect was rather like a species of musical hot-water bottle, a rubbery gurgle interspersed with the occasional damp belch. To make anything of it would require someone of rare abilities, a near-genius, and eventually one appeared. This was Coleman Hawkins.

Hawkins found a voice within the tenor saxophone – an urgent, passionate, rhapsodic voice which can be heard in recordings with Fletcher Henderson's band from the mid-twenties to 1934, and also on a famous record by the Mound City Blues Blowers of 1929 – *One Hour* and *Hello Lola*. Because he was the first great tenor saxophonist, everyone more or less copied him. In the course of ten years he had made the instrument into a major jazz voice and was revered, not only in America but in Europe too. In 1934 he visited England, as a guest of Jack Hylton's orchestra, and so ecstatic was his reception that he stayed for five years.

He returned in 1939 and recorded his masterpiece, *Body And Soul*. Alongside his immensely authoritative tone and delivery he possessed a superb ear for harmony, and in *Body And Soul* he methodically dismantles the tune into its harmonic components and reassembles it, complete with a wonderful array of passing chords and substitutions. The original melody is in there somewhere, but only as a kind of cowering presence.

It was because of his fascination with harmony that Hawkins, of all the musicians of his generation, was the one to understand the new bebop style. He encouraged the young players, like Gillespie, and even used them on his records as early as 1944.

He continued playing with all his old cunning but gradually a kind of brusque impatience began to creep into his solos, as though he couldn't really be bothered to go into it all again, night after night. Always a drinker, he ended up living on little more than brandy. By the time of his death in 1969, he gave the impression of a man who had simply got bored with life, and even with his art.

Jack TEAGARDEN

b. 29 August 1905
d. 15 January 1964

Amiable, relaxed, even lazy – that is the impression Jack Teagarden gives in his film appearances. Most celebrated of these is his *Rockin' Chair* duet with Louis Armstrong, captured at its ripest in the 1958 documentary *Jazz On A Summer's Day*. But that is Teagarden the singer and occasional actor.

As a trombonist, he is considered to be one of the few white musicians ever to play the blues with complete natural authority and assurance. He is certainly the first to have done so on record. It was partly because he grew up in a part of Texas where relations between the races were comparatively unstrained. As a child he loved to listen to the music of travelling bands and the singing of black congregations at revival meetings. The blues, therefore, was part of his native language. Teagarden's whole approach to music was one of rhythmic ease. In the mid-twenties, when Louis Armstrong was teaching the rest of the world the fundamentals of swing, of creating a melodic line that flowed over and through the beat, instead of jumping up and down *with* it, Teagarden seems already to have grasped the idea. He also had a fluid, slippery technique on an instrument which does not invite nimble execution.

When he arrived in New York, in 1927, he was instantly accepted as a leading player and for the rest of his life had a busy career. He was much in demand for recording sessions, especially with small pick-up groups made up of rising jazzmen of the time. Typical of these was the Venuti-Lang All-Stars of 1931, a band which included the young Benny Goodman on clarinet and Teagarden's brother Charlie on trumpet. The loosely-knit format of sessions such as these brought out the casual elegance of his trombone style to perfection. After five years with Paul Whiteman in the mid-thirties, Teagarden formed his own big band and then, in 1946, he joined Louis Armstrong's All-Stars.

Armstrong had also given up trying to keep a big band together; the relief of both at being able to concentrate simply on playing imparts a wonderfully free and unbuttoned air to the first All-Stars records. The famous 1947 live recording from New York Town Hall sums up the spirit of the band perfectly. It also includes the first of many versions of *Rockin' Chair*, the song which symbolizes the close and unaffected friendship between the two men.

After a few years Teagarden left the All-Stars, to lead a series of small bands and take to the road with various combinations of top soloists. It was with one of these – under the nominal leadership of Eddie Condon – that I heard him in person, at a London concert some time in the late fifties. The most memorable moment of the show was Teagarden's solo on the slow blues; he removed the bell section of the trombone and replaced it with a glass tumbler, to act as a kind of mute. The result was a plaintive, keening, infinitely melancholy sound.

Teagarden died in 1964, at the age of 59. He was still at the height of his powers, but it had been a fulfilled and rewarding life.

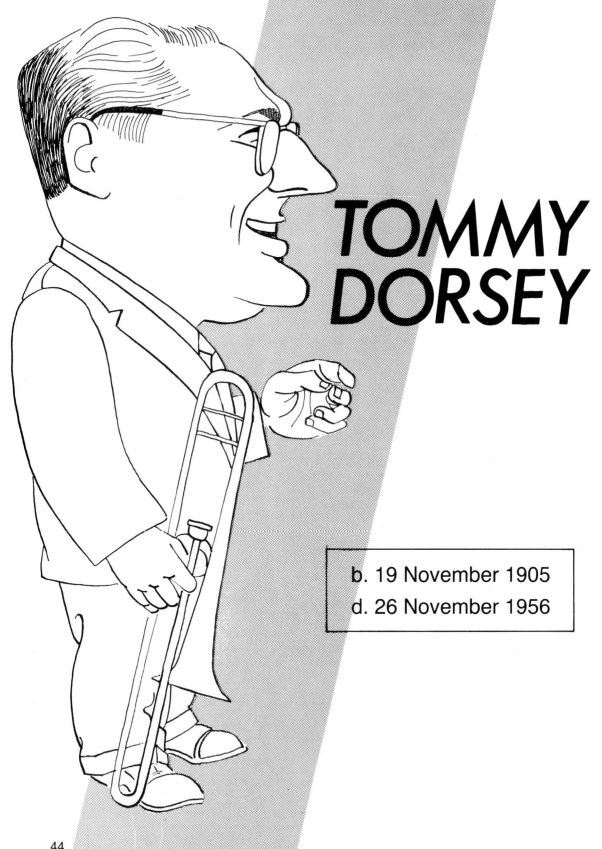

TOMMY DORSEY

b. 19 November 1905
d. 26 November 1956

The big swing bands of the late thirties and early forties provided mass entertainment in the huge dance halls across the United States; they were also heard over the radio in the remotest corners of the land. Indeed, the radio was a much stronger force than records in disseminating popular music.

Each band had its own style: some were dreamy and sentimental, some raucous and exciting. The Tommy Dorsey Orchestra was typical of the first-division big band of the period.

Starting out as a jazz trumpet and trombone player in the twenties, he played in the same milieu as Goodman and Teagarden – pick-up recording groups and ad hoc dance bands. He was a member of Paul Whiteman's orchestra and later formed a band with his saxophonist brother, Jimmy. Both Dorseys were quick-tempererd and quarrelsome men, and the Dorsey Brothers' Orchestra soon gained an awesome reputation as a kind of travelling battlefield.

In 1935 they belatedly realized this was no way for grown men to behave; they broke up the band, and each formed his own. Tommy's became the more successful and remained in business into the 1950s. Its speciality was Tommy's trombone playing – high, smooth and seamless – in ballads, such as his signature tune *I'm Getting Sentimental Over You*. Like most others, the Dorsey orchestra included a 'band-within-a-band', a small jazz group which would be featured during each show. His was called the Clambake Seven; it included whichever jazz soloists the band contained at the time and acted as a counterbalance to the slightly soupy romanticism.

It is almost impossible to find a musician of note who did not pass through one or more of the big bands. Dorsey at one time or another employed Buddy Rich, Gene Krupa, Buddy De Franco, Bunny Berigan, Charlie Shavers and Joe Bushkin. And from the big bands came the people who were eventually to replace them, the star vocalists, the arrangers who created their settings, the musical directors and producers of the revitalized post-war music industry.

EARL HINES

With his extraordinary wig, made apparently out of textured toffee, his ever-present cigar and loudly checked jackets, Earl Hines, in his latter days, looked for all the world like an escapee from a Damon Runyon story.

This, combined with a stage manner better adapted to a medicine show than a nightclub or concert hall, sometimes misled casual onlookers to assume that he was some kind of aged comic. In fact, he was one of the half-dozen greatest pianists in jazz history, with a musical mind of remarkable subtlety and a technique which seemed to get more and more dazzling as he grew older.

If 'Fatha', as he was affectionately called, had retired or fallen under a bus as early as 1930 his name would still be in the jazz Pantheon. Historically, he was the man who finally liberated the jazz piano from the apron strings of ragtime, whose brilliant accompaniments goaded the young Louis Armstrong into accepting the challenge of his own genius and embarking on a solo career.

Hines first came to the notice of the jazz world in 1928, when his recorded duet with Armstrong, entitled *Weatherbird*, was released. It contains all the elements of his later style – particularly a technique of playing the melody and variations in octaves in the right hand, and ending each phrase with a tiny tremolo, just like Armstrong's vibrato. For more than fifty years Hines's 'trumpet-style' has been one of the most imitated in jazz.

His extrovert style and perfect judgement in picking musicians made him a natural bandleader. At one time in the early 1940s, his band contained both Dizzy Gillespie and Charlie Parker and its singer was Billy Eckstine. Needing someone to fill in on piano while he entertained the customers, he hired the young unknown Sarah Vaughan for the job.

When he began visiting Britain in the 1960s we saw at first hand just how extraordinary his musical powers were. One occasionally came across dazed bass players who had not quite recovered from the experience of being taken on a guided tour of the Hines harmonic universe.

As Count Basie once remarked, 'If you run up against Earl, you're likely to get bruised.'

b. 28 December 1905
d. 22 April 1983

BENNY CARTER

b. 8 August 1907

Benny Carter is nearly 80; when I saw him last year he looked a well preserved 60, dapper, amiable and displaying a kind of old-fashioned courtesy. His main instrument is the alto saxophone, and he plays not only the usual 'doubles' – clarinet etc – but also the trumpet, as well as dabbling with the piano. For most of his life he has made the bulk of his living as a composer and arranger, in recent years writing extensively for films and television.

It is extremely rare to play both brass and reed instruments because they require completely different *embouchure*, or blowing technique, and the use of different sets of muscles. Carter is unique because he is one of the greatest alto players in jazz history, whose instrumental control and beauty of sound is always remarked upon, and at the same time a trumpeter good enough to be hired by the best. If you ever see the old Lena Horne movie *Stormy Weather* you will see Benny Carter being Fats Waller's trumpet player; in *The Snows of Kilimanjaro* you will also see Benny Carter

being the alto saxophonist in an early fifties Paris nightclub. He's perfect in both roles.

He played with most of the leading black bands of the twenties and early thirties – Fletcher Henderson, McKinney's Cottonpickers, the Chocolate Dandies, even, briefly, with Ellington – and soon gained a reputation for being mildly superhuman. His saxophone playing, too, had a kind of Olympian detachment. The word used then and ever afterwards about it was 'elegant'. Carter's elegance, his poise and self-assurance, the unruffled, creamy surface of his sound, was not always in favour with critics of grittier tastes, but it captivated musicians. Among those who fell for it was the English musician (and, incidentally, critic) Spike Hughes, who travelled to New York in 1933 to record some of his own compositions with a black American band, and chose Carter to organize it. The results, under the name of 'Spike Hughes and his Negro Orchestra', were superb, and Carter was soon invited to Europe on the strength of them.

From 1935 to 1938 he lived on this side of the Atlantic, and for almost a year acted as staff arranger to Henry Hall's BBC orchestra. His European recordings, especially those with Coleman Hawkins and Django Reinhardt in Paris, are among the best he ever made. Since the mid-forties he has lived in Hollywood, writing his scores, with occasional forays into performing – as much for his own enjoyment, it seems, as anything else.

49

Stephane GRAPPELLI

b. 26 January 1908

It would be difficult to imagine a more oddly matched pair than Django Reinhardt and Stephane Grappelli – the one an illiterate, impulsive, spendthrift gypsy, the other a model of Parisian *savoir-faire*. Uneasy though this extraordinary partnership always was, it was the basis of a band which produced the first convincing example of non-American jazz; the Quintette du Hot Club de France succeeded in being at the same time unmistakably jazz and unmistakably Gallic. The Quintette's classic records, made between 1934 and 1939, owe their charm to the precarious balance between Grappelli's melting lightness and Reinhardt's sinuous urgency and bravura technique.

STEPHANE GRAPPELLI

The original Quintette broke up in 1939, and Django died in 1953, but Stephane Grappelli continued to play and develop. A careful man, he looked after himself and began to reach his creative peak in his sixties. He has always possessed the remarkable ability to skate along the edge of sentimentality without actually falling in, and his work with the Quintette proves how effectively he can swing. But Grappelli's playing in old age has assumed a wonderful new luxuriance. With almost negligent ease, he explores melodic ideas in long, curving lines, makes little musical jokes in passing, or opens up his tone to play a simple, sparsely decorated tune.

The rising curve of Stephane Grappelli's career at a time of life when most men have decided to quit is without parallel in jazz. He has toured the world and played alongside the greatest artists. Some of his best records in recent years have been made with musicians young enough to be his grandchildren, notably a splendid album, *Paris Encounter*, with Gary Burton.

DJANGO REINHARDT

Django was a gypsy of the Manouche tribe and was born in Belgium, because that's where his mother's caravan happened to be at the time. At the age of 18 he almost died in a caravan fire, and his left hand was so badly burned that everyone who saw it assumed that the young man's guitar-playing days were over. However, he worked out a complete new technique for himself, using his two good fingers and thumb.

Although he can have heard very little jazz until he was grown up, Reinhardt took to it at once and seemed to have a complete instinctive understanding of swing and jazz phraseology. Throughout the thirties, whenever an American band came to France, Django was the first person the musicians went looking for. He recorded with many of them, notably Coleman Hawkins and Dickie Wells, and acquired an enormous reputation as a result. He is the only non-American musician ever to have been a major influence on the development of jazz.

Django REINHARDT

b. 23 January 1910

d. 16 May 1953

51

High among the popular archetypes of the swing era was the frantic, gum-chewing drummer, perched up at the very apex of the stage set, in the full glare of the spotlight. The model for this image is Gene Krupa. He was by no means the best big band drummer, but he knew how to make the hitherto unspectacular business of playing the drums into a complete show. His eyes would glaze in the manner of one possessed, his hair would fall forward over his face, his tie would be loosened, he would sweat profusely. At the end of his big feature number he would collapse, panting over the kit, like a sprinter who had just breasted the tape. He had a great act. Useless to point out that, beside Basie's Jo Jones, Krupa

was somewhat heavy and unimaginative, or that Ellington's Sonny Greer could do all the same tricks with half the effort. When Gene Krupa, as a star of the Benny Goodman Orchestra, went into his tom-tom routine in *Sing Sing Sing* he brought the house down, and that was that.

To be fair, when Krupa left Goodman and formed his own band in 1938 he proved a model bandleader and by no means the selfish, grandstanding performer that he might have been. He employed Roy Eldridge as featured trumpet soloist, an association which proved difficult because of Eldridge's position as the only black musician in a white band – and his female vocalist was Anita O'Day, later to become a leading singer of the bebop years. His own playing improved, too. During his later life, when he travelled with 'Jazz At The Philharmonic', his playing had acquired a litheness and lift which had not been there during his period as a pop idol.

GENE KRUPA

b. 15 January 1909
d. 16 October 1973

Lionel HAMPTON

b. 12 April 1909

The vibraphone is a delicate, tinkling instrument, the last thing you would expect a forceful person like Lionel Hampton to choose. But, although he has led some of the most riotously exciting big bands in jazz history, Hampton is a musician of enormous resourcefulness, and treats the instrument in many different ways: as a huge keyboard (which it is) on which to create dazzling harmonic and melodic patterns, or as percussion (which it also is) upon which he can beat out a rhythmic tattoo.

As a very young man he was a percussionist playing in the West Coast recording studios. On one session, Louis Armstrong took a fancy to the sound of a vibraphone which Hampton was doodling around with and got him to play a solo on *Memories Of You*; that was the start not only of Hamp's true career but also of the vibraphone as a jazz instrument. When he joined Benny Goodman in 1936, as a kind of permanent guest artist (like Teddy Wilson), the world at large became aware of the instrument and how it could be made to swing. The urgency of Hamp's playing on up-tempo numbers with Goodman contrasts delightfully with Wilson's polished ease. At the same period, Hampton was organizing sessions of his own, featuring as many leading players of the day as he could grab, for Victor Records.

The activities of those four years (1936–40) established Lionel Hampton as a major jazz artist. What he did afterwards gave him a reputation as a showman-bandleader which sometimes distressed more sober jazz lovers. The band would play flat out for most of the time, with Hampton invariably playing a feature number that ended with his jumping up and down on a huge drum.

But, at the same time, he could drop back instantly into his lyrical, reflective style and play with immense authority and imagination. This has certainly been the case when he has found himself in challenging musical company, notably in his recordings with Art Tatum and Stan Getz.

In 1953 Hampton took the big band to Europe for a tour and struck up a quite remarkable love affair between himself and the French public. For over thirty years Lionel Hampton has been a star in France, with a popularity far beyond that of the biggest jazz names. His effusive, outgoing personality seems to appeal to the Gallic sensibility and, even in his seventies, he has only to walk on to a French stage to cause instant uproar.

Benny Goodman

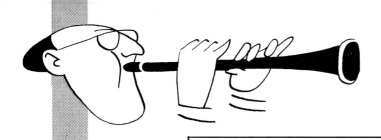

b. 30 May 1909
d. 13 June 1986

One August night in 1935 the patrons at the Palomar Ballroom, Los Angeles, stopped dancing and crowded around the bandstand to cheer Benny Goodman's orchestra. It was the beginning of the swing era, and of Goodman's reign as King of Swing.

Although he was only 26 at the time, Benny Goodman had already been a professional clarinettist for half his life, and there is something curiously middle-aged about the photographs of him taken during his heyday. The big band made him rich and famous, as he had intended it to, but Goodman the jazz musician is heard to best advantage in small-group recordings. Almost from the beginning the orchestra featured spots for Goodman with a trio or quartet, the first with Teddy Wilson at the piano and the second adding Lionel Hampton on vibraphone. It was quite bold, in the late thirties, for a white bandleader to include black musicians, but Goodman never bowed for a moment to pressure in this matter. However, despite this, he was never held in great affection by the musicians who worked for him. From the cold gleam behind those owlish spectacles you could see that he was never one of the boys. When, many years later, Goodman toured the USSR with an all-star band, Zoot Sims was asked what it had been like to play in Russia. '*Every* gig with Benny is like playing in Russia,' Zoot replied.

Perhaps the most superb small band Goodman ever led was his septet, featuring Basie, Charlie Christian and Cootie Williams, in 1940. Here Goodman really showed what a superb player he was – not, as his character might suggest, coldly precise but ferocious and passionate.

When the big bands collapsed in the late forties Goodman did not seem unduly worried. He had been dabbling with classical music for some time, and now conveyed the general impression that his mind was on higher things, such as Mozart and Brahms, with jazz as a kind of harmless relaxation. Between that time and his death on 13 June 1986, he formed numerous temporary bands, some of them superb, and gradually turned into an institution.

LESTER YOUNG

b. 27 August 1909
d. 15 March 1959

Among the really great and influential jazz musicians – the Armstrongs, the Ellingtons, the Coltranes – Lester Young is the one whose name is almost totally unknown to the general public. The reason is that, unlike Armstrong he had no show, unlike Ellington he did not have the glamour of being a bandleader and unlike Coltrane he died too soon to benefit from the elevation of jazz from the status of entertainment to that of art.

Lester Young was a shy, intensely private man who first recorded in 1936, at the relatively advanced age of 27, when he was a member of Count Basie's orchestra. That first session, with a small group from the band, produced two performances which completely upset the orthodox idea of what a tenor saxophone should sound like. Light, airy, mercurial, Lester's whole approach was the opposite of Hawkins's massive gravity. There were some at the time who refused to take it seriously, but by the time Basie's band had become established Lester Young was its star soloist, and the

jazz tenor saxophone tradition had acquired the duality which it retains to this day: there are Hawkins players and there are Lester players (Coltrane, for instance, was a Hawkins player).

There is no more consistently perfect body of recorded work in jazz than that which Lester Young created between 1936 and 1941 – with the Basie band, with Billie Holiday, with various small groups such as the Kansas City Seven. At the time Billie Holiday gave him the nickname 'Prez' – short for The President – and such was his eminence that the name stuck to him for ever.

Lester left Basie at the end of 1940 and, for reasons which are still the subject of speculation, his playing changed. It used to be claimed that his time in the US Army (most of which was spent in Detention Barracks) was the cause of his new, slower, more melancholy style, but this cannot be true, because the change began before the army claimed him.

In the last fifteen years of his life, Prez developed yet another voice – laconic, fragile and immensely moving. Of all jazz musicians, he is the one whose playing most transparently echoes his own feelings. His medium in these final years was American song; he listened avidly to singers – Sinatra, Dick Haymes etc – and strove to create a kind of instrumental equivalent to their minute subtlety. 'You have to know the *words*', he would insist. This was greeted with universal incomprehension, and he died in 1959 believing his life to have been a failure.

ARTIE SHAW

b. 23 May 1910

Artie Shaw walked away from success, not once but repeatedly. His was one of the biggest names of the swing era, his orchestra one of the strongest draws and his clarinet playing reckoned by many to be superior to anyone's. His hit record, *Begin The Beguine*, is still used today to sum up the atmosphere of the late thirties. Yet, in 1939 Shaw simply gave up bandleading and withdrew temporarily from the public eye. The reason, as he has explained since, was that he found the whole business of being an entertainer boring and the behaviour of teenage fans intolerable.

The musician in Artie Shaw could never come to terms with the fairground aspect of showbusiness. His ambition had always been towards writing, and he claimed only to have become a bandleader in order to earn enough money to complete his education. But he was also a superb player, with an inimitable tone – dark and plangent – and an unrivalled technique. It is something of a paradox that this fastidiousness and perfectionism went along with a public image as a Hollywood Romeo. Three of his eight wives were film stars – Ava Gardner, Lana Turner and Evelyn Keyes – and his picture was rarely absent for long from the glossy magazines.

In 1942 he again broke up his band, this time to join the US Navy. Given a hand-picked band to lead, he demanded to be sent to the Pacific war zone and toured there, more or less constantly under fire, for 18 months. Medically discharged, he put together yet another band, again highly successful, got fed up and devoted a year to studying classical music.

He wrote a uniquely self-aware autobiography, *The Trouble with Cinderella*, and continued playing intermittently until the mid-fifties, when he moved to Spain. There he designed his own hilltop house and wrote a novel, *I Love You, I Hate You, Drop Dead*, whose title has been construed as a perfect summing-up of his attitude to the American public.

At the time of writing Artie Shaw is 75 years old and working on another novel. A man of enormous intelligence and extraordinary powers of application, he has successfully operated a dairy farm, a gun-manufacturing business and a film distribution company. An excellent two-hour film biography, *Time Is All You've Got*, directed by Brigitte Berman, was made in 1985.

ART TATUM

b. 13 October 1910

d. 5 November 1956

Somebody came up to Fats Waller, when he was playing in a nightclub, and told him that Art Tatum had just walked in. Fats stopped playing and announced, 'Ladies and gentleman, your attention please. God is in the house!' That is how pianists all seem to regard Art Tatum. The rest of the world takes a slightly more moderate view, but there is no doubt that Tatum was a virtuoso of stupendous technical powers. During the forties, when he was pretty well resident in the clubs along New York's 52nd Street, some unlikely figures could be seen frequenting the dives from time to time: Horowitz, Toscanini and Gieseking were among the classical masters who came to wonder at this pianistic phenomenon.

Art Tatum was, to all intents and purposes, blind. His whole life consisted of music; he had been a child prodigy, with his own radio show at the age of 15. His style was, at bottom, a form of stride piano, and he acknowledged Fats Waller as his greatest influence. However, on top of the steady left hand he piled increasingly complex runs and arpeggios, until the original tune was submerged in thousands of glittering notes. The runs would suddenly change direction, too, or cut across the beat. To liven things up even further, Tatum made a habit of suddenly changing the key – usually just for a couple of bars, until the listener's ear had adjusted, then he changed it back again. He also altered the harmonic sequences of well known tunes, such as *I Got Rhythm* – a practice which made him a favourite with younger musicians of the Gillespie – Parker generation.

Tatum played mainly as a soloist, or with accompanying bass and guitar. Despite what many critics have claimed, he was a perfectly good band pianist, especially in his earlier years, but it is as a solo performer that he worked best. Like all pianists who make their living playing in nightclubs, he possessed an enormous repertoire, and in the early fifties he recorded a staggering *eleven* albums in a few days, with brief halts for sleep.

This series, entitled *The Solo Masterpieces*, was followed by another, *The Group Masterpieces*, in which he was joined by a number of eminent players. The best of these are the ones in which the other player either phrases as simply as possible (Ben

Webster) or gives Tatum a run for his money (Buddy De Franco).

Among the pianists who have admitted a debt to Art Tatum are Nat Cole and Oscar Peterson, but his influence can be found everywhere, not just in technique but in the whole approach of modern pianists to harmony.

Brilliant, exciting, occasionally chaotic and even slightly manic at times, Roy 'Little Jazz' Eldridge is a complete original. Historically he stands midway between Louis Armstrong and Dizzy Gillespie, an essential link in the great jazz trumpet tradition.

As a young man he was influenced more by saxophonists than by other trumpet players, and the speed and fluency of his playing reflects this. Before the advent of his disciple Gillespie, he was probably the most technically accomplished trumpeter in jazz. The charm of Eldridge's solos lies partly in their sheer unpredictability. When a good idea occurs to him he immediately gives chase, no matter what line of thought he has been pursuing – a practice which results in some gloriously incongruous effects, with slow ballads suddenly breaking into a gallop and subdued mid-range solos sprouting alarming high-register shrieks.

So eminent had Eldridge become by the mid-thirties that he was asked to join two white bands – those of Gene Krupa and Artie Shaw – as featured soloist. This was in the days when racially mixed bands were almost unheard of, and when black and white people in America still lived almost totally segregated lives. The bitter experience of travelling with Krupa and Shaw, despite the strenuous support of his fellow musicians, stayed with Eldridge ever afterwards and it made him socially a very cautious man.

Eldridge formed his own big band in 1944, which was exactly the wrong moment to do so, when rising costs, wartime restrictions and changes in public taste were finally closing down the swing era. He had two goes at it, in 1944 and 1946, lost his shirt on both occasions and claimed never to have regretted it for a minute.

After that he worked with small groups and as a world-travelling soloist, his effervescence subsiding slightly as the years passed, but always a vastly impressive player. Following a heart attack in 1980 he virtually retired from music.

ROY ELDRIDGE

b. 30 January 1911

b. 18 May 1911
d. 24 November 1985

'Big Joe', as he was known, was not just very fat or very tall, but huge in all respects. From this immense frame issued a voice of similar proportions, a sort of controlled bellow which was, in fact, perfect for the simple declamation of blues phrases against a swing or boogie beat – the style actually known as 'blues shouting' – and it had at its centre an oily, wheedling lewdness that was all his own.

Big Joe's blues were mostly about love – or, more correctly, sex – and the remainder were about food and drink. To call them basic is putting it mildly. His variation on the timeless theme of 'Gather ye rosebuds' was: 'Baby, you're so beautiful but you gotta die some day. All I want's a little lovin' before you pass away.'

There is reasonable case for claiming that he invented rock 'n' roll; at least, he used the phrase often in the early fifties. He never got to be the idol of teenagers, but lack of pop success didn't upset him in the least, and he soon gained a loyal following among jazz followers, particularly after the release in 1956 of a superb album called *Boss Of The Blues*.

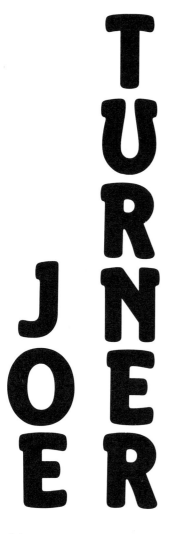

Stan Kenton

b. 19 February 1912
d. 25 August 1979

'Progressive Jazz' was the label Stan Kenton devised to describe his idiosyncratic type of big band music, although others had less complimentary names. The typical Kenton piece is massive, with great blocks of sound colliding like the crack of doom, and very little of the ease and simplicity normally considered essential to a good jazz performance. And yet Kenton formed his first band in 1941 (which was late in the day) and kept it going for thirty years, as the giants of the swing era collapsed all around. Like extinct species of animals, the swing bands died because their habitat, the ballroom, contracted to a point at which it could no longer support life. Kenton's band found that it could live in a new habitat, the world of the concert platform. And, with everyone sitting down to listen, the emphasis shifted from swing to sound.

The title of Kenton's gargantuan 42-piece touring orchestra of 1950–51, *Innovations In Modern Music*, sums up his approach. It suggested the new age of science and progress. This music proved extremely popular with college audiences, who were thrilled by its sheer volume and dissonance and by the pretentious titles and general air of being in the cultural *avant-garde*.

In retrospect, Kenton's best pieces were the ones that got away – the exuberant bebop of *How High The Moon* and the clear, simple lines of Gerry Mulligan's composition *Young Blood*. These are not Progressive Jazz, they're just jazz, and all the better for it.

b. 13 May 1912

Gil Evans is a great master of orchestration. He can write a phrase for piccolo and tuba and convince you that you're hearing all the ghostly harmonies in between. His vast, sumptuous settings for Miles Davis (*Miles Ahead, Porgy and Bess, Sketches of Spain*), recorded in the late fifties, are packed with examples of this strange alchemy. They also demonstrate his understanding of Miles Davis's style, a sympathy that comes close to telepathy at times.

It was Duke Ellington who said that the jazz composer must know how a man plays poker before he can write for him, and that is exactly Gil Evans's strength. On *Porgy and Bess*, for instance, there is a piece called *Gone*, which is a kind of mini-concerto for drummer Philly Joe Jones. Now, Philly Joe was a man with a highly distinctive set of mannerisms, and the whole arrangement is built in such a way that each of its high-points turns out to be a typical Philly Joe-ism.

The words 'composer' and 'arranger' get hopelessly tangled in jazz use, because the difference is so insignificant. A 'composition' uses an original theme, while an 'arrangement' takes one that already exists and – well – rearranges. Gil Evans, like most musicians of his age, began working with the big dance bands of the thirties and forties. He was staff arranger with the Claude Thornhill Orchestra, and his job was to write versions of new or well known tunes in the band's recognizable style – a style which he had helped to create. The habit of reworking other people's themes proved tenacious, and some of Evans's most ambitious compositions are, strictly speaking, 'arrangements' – including, of course, *Porgy and Bess*.

He takes as basic material themes from an enormous span of popular music – from Jelly Roll Morton's *King Porter Stomp* to Jimi Hendrix's *Little Wing*. One of his most impressive reworkings is a long version of Kurt Weill's *Barbara Song*, in which the instrumental textures change like cloud formations, slowly altering their patterns of light and shade.

In the past decade, Gil Evans has travelled the world, sometimes with his own band and sometimes taking charge of musicians he does not know particularly well. This should be where the jazz composer comes unstuck, according to the Ellingtonian dictum, but he manages to bring off quite extraordinary feats by virtue of his instinct for the essentials of someone's style. I saw him once rehearsing an international band in Berlin. So international was it that his instructions sometimes had to go through two stages of translation (e.g. English to German to Serbo-Croat), but the end result was coherent and exciting.

Gil Evans is like Ellington in one significant way: his music has been changing constantly for almost half a century, and yet none of it could possibly be the work of anyone else.

Gil
Evans

TEDDY WILSON

b. 24 November 1912

Assured, tasteful, urbane – Teddy Wilson's piano style has been part of jazz music for half a century. He is one of the great accompanists, a great fashioner of perfect introductions and apt comments on the side, and a superb leader of small bands. His position as organizer of the classic Billie Holiday sessions of the late thirties has tended to obscure the fact that he also directed innumerable other sessions during this period, featuring Mildred Bailey and others, not one of them less than successful and most outstandingly good. He was also a member of the Benny Goodman Trio, by no means the first mixed-race band in jazz, but the first to take a high profile.

Teddy Wilson was one of the first academically trained musicians in jazz. He studied for four years at Tuskagee Institute. Even as an established professional he continued to take lessons, and was a friend of the young Leonard Bernstein in the forties. Academic connections of this kind were almost unheard of for jazz players until the mid-fifties. This grounding allowed Wilson to move around easily in a music profession which was still quite strictly segregated, with black musicians denied access to other kinds of work.

This sober career profile does not, however, point to a player of anonymous technical efficiency. Teddy Wilson's style is as recognizable as that of any pianist in jazz, and full of subdued passion. It derives originally from Earl Hines, whose early solos Wilson learned to play by heart as a boy, and from Art Tatum. Tatum's influence can be picked up in some of the slippery descending runs that turn up from time to time but, typically, they seem to be dropped in as self-effacingly as possible.

As he became more of a celebrity, Teddy Wilson played less and less as an accompanist and more as a soloist, or leader of a trio. Many of his later records have been elegant and fastidious versions of classic American songs, and betray a particular fondness for pieces by Gershwin and Cole Porter.

WOODY HERMAN

b. 16 May 1913

Woody Herman is one of those rare birds in jazz, the unselfish bandleader. Only Art Blakey can beat him when it comes to naming great jazz musicians who had their first exposure with his band, and he always gives the impression of being so delighted with what the players are doing that he's forgotten to play anything himself. In point of fact, Woody is a very accomplished clarinettist, and when he does decide to play the results are always splendid.

But it is the bands – the 'Herman Herds' – that will be his greatest contribution to jazz. The First Herd, subtitled 'The Band That Plays The Blues', was a late entry in the swing-era stakes, but got off to a good start with the 1939 hit record *Woodchoppers' Ball*. Like all Herman's bands, it had a nucleus of highly individual soloists: trombonist Bill Harris, trumpeter Sonny Berman, saxophonist Flip Phillips. In almost half a century of changing personnel the sound of Herman's band has been dictated by the styles of the musicians he has chosen.

The Second, Herd, formed in 1947, was undoubtedly the most influential of all the bands. Its masterpiece, *Four Brothers*, a composition by Jimmy Guiffre, featured the cool tenor saxophone sound which was to be universally copied in the succeeding decade and a half, played by Stan Getz, Zoot Sims, Herbie Steward and Serge Chaloff. Getz and Sims, in particular, made their first mark with Herman.

The difficulty of keeping a big band together during the fifties forced Woody to use smaller groups from time to time, but sometimes these proved to be every bit as good. The group known as the 'Las Vegas Herd' made a prodigiously swinging album in 1955, entitled *Jackpot*, which demonstrated how intelligent arrangements and strong soloists could make eight instruments sound like at least twice that number.

The Third and Fourth Herds are rather difficult to define, because the line-up kept changing so fast, but the 1963 band was certainly a classic. I shall never forget hearing it at the Metropole Café in New York, spread out on a long, narrow stage behind the bar and almost blistering the paintwork with its fiercely accurate ensemble and the bravura solo playing of trumpeter Bill Chase and saxophonist Sal Nistico.

Billie Holiday

b. 7 April 1915

d. 17 July 1959

Despite the title of her autobiography, and the fatuous film version of it – *Lady Sings The Blues* – Billie Holiday was not a blues singer. This is one of many popular misconceptions. She was a supreme artist *not* because she was rejected by her father, was brought up in a brothel, became a drug addict, went to jail, was exploited by men, had a violent temper and got arrested on her deathbed. All these things are true but, in the end, irrelevant. Billie Holiday's achievement was to take American songs, purge them of sentimentality and raise them to expressive heights unimagined by their composers. She had the techniques and instincts of a jazz musician, and she is both the greatest jazz singer and the greatest interpreter of American song.

Billie was never as popular as Sinatra or Crosby and died too young to grow into a *diva*, like Ella Fitzgerald or Sarah Vaughan. Her earliest and best work was so undramatic and obscurely produced it went largely unnoticed, and when she did finally achieve a measure of fame it was tainted with notoriety.

Many of Billie's early records were made for use in juke boxes. The idea was to turn out lively versions of current pop songs, as cheaply as possible. The critic and record producer John Hammond decided to record informal sessions with some of the jazz musicians who constantly passed through New York with the leading big bands and the pianist Teddy Wilson organized these sessions. In the late thirties the cream of the swing era would check in to pick up the 20 dollar fee for a few enjoyable hours' music making; Billie was often there and so was Lester Young. The duets between Billie's voice and Lester's tenor saxophone on numbers such as *Me, Myself and I, A Sailboat In The Moonlight* and *I Must Have That Man* are among the highest masterpieces in jazz.

Billie was then a robust young woman, although inclined to be touchy and grossly unreliable. It was in the early forties that she was taken up by the intelligentsia and characterized in magazine articles as a victim, a wronged woman. Her repertoire changed to doom-laden ballads, string sections took the place of the small jazz group, and she found people writing songs especially for her. But the priceless gift of rhythmic transformation and melodic purity was called upon less and less. By now she really *was* a victim – of heroin and the first in a series of utterly despicable men.

Following her spell in jail for narcotics possession in 1947–48, Billie Holiday's audiences came increasingly to look like voyeurs. Everyone knew she wore the long white gloves to cover the needle-marks; her voice sounded cracked and ageing. And yet, given half a chance, she could still transform a song. Another series of small-band records, made in the mid-fifties is full of examples – *Day In, Day Out, Let's Call The Whole Thing Off*, and a sublime version of Ellington's *Sophisticated Lady*. But her singing seriously declined in her last few years; the many recordings from nightclubs and concerts tell the unhappy truth.

FRANK SINATRA

b. 12 December 1915

What's he doing here? Well, he has featured in jazz polls for decades, starting with the Down Beat readers' poll in 1942. He began as a band singer, first with Harry James and then with Tommy Dorsey, and made some superb records with Count Basie in the sixties – and Lester Young nominated him as vocalist with his 'dream band'. So you can't say that Frank Sinatra has no connection with jazz. Of course, he has connections with all kinds of other things as well, but that's beside the point.

Some time in the late sixties Sinatra appeared with Basie at the Newport Jazz Festival and some people actually complained. Perhaps they didn't like the fact that he was rich and famous, perhaps they didn't like his politics – but if they were objecting to Sinatra as a vocalist, then they were demonstrating their own misunderstanding of jazz.

The aspect of Frank Sinatra that jazz listeners (and musicians) find irresistible is his phrasing, especially at swing tempos. His great period as a singer runs from 1954 to the early sixties, the period of his Capitol and Reprise albums – *Songs For Swinging Lovers, Come Fly with Me, Ring-a-Ding-Ding* and about twenty more. Taken together they add up to a demonstration of the art of singing classic American song, which is, after all, the basic material of most jazz musicians' work. He knows how to make a tune swing with the minimum of fuss and the maximum of grace.

Sinatra almost never alters a song; he doesn't add notes, radically shift the rhythms, substitute notes or incorporate scat choruses. He sings it almost straight – but the important part is the *almost*. The tiniest hesitation, a little

push here and a lagging beat there, turns a pleasant melody into a beautiful one. It's a subtle technique, a question of rhythmic poise, and it is one which jazz musicians recognize immediately. To play the melody and make it your own — that's the final achievement. Louis Armstrong could do it — Lester Young, Art Pepper, Jack Teagarden, even John Coltrane could do it. And that's what Sinatra can do. Will you ever be able to hear *I Thought About You* or *Day In, Day Out* without the echo of his voice in the background?

Slim Gaillard

b. 4 January 1916

Because styles of humour age so quickly, the art of Slim Gaillard is irrevocably trapped in the 1940s. Most of the hip catch phrases of the period derived from his private jive-talk language, a scrambled, surrealistic jargon which he called 'Vout'. The songs he made up were of the nonsense-syllables kind, and his musical style was choppy, four-in-a-bar swing.

His records have the charm of perfect period pieces. Generations of jazz fans have fallen for the *Avocado Seed Soup Symphony* or the outrageous *Chicken Rhythm*, which consists of a common obscenity, thinly disguised as the clucking of a chicken and chanted over the bass line of *I Got Rhythm*.

In 1944 he recorded the now famous ses-sion featuring the very young Charlie Parker ('Yardbird Oroonie') and Dizzy Gillespie ('Daz McSkivens Vout Oroonie') in works like *The Flat Foot Floogie* and *Poppity Pop*. He also appears, with his one-time partner Slam Stewart ('Slim and Slam'), in Olsen and Johnson's crazy film, *Helzapoppin*. During their cameo performance Slim produces one of his party pieces – playing the piano with the backs of his fingers.

In the early fifties Slim gave up performing and became a film extra, going on to play small character parts. He appeared in the television series *Roots*. Dizzy persuaded him, in 1980, to return to the trade of jazz jester: 'Go to Europe, man. They *know* you there!' Slim took his advice and discovered that he was not only known but adored.

NAT KING COLE

b. 17 March 1917

d. 15 February 1965

If Nat Cole had not been such a tremendously good jazz pianist his turning into a ballad singer would not have upset jazz lovers quite so much. But the facts are undeniable: in the early 1940s Nat Cole was *the* up-and-coming jazz pianist, winner of awards, leader of an admired trio, one of the best rhythm-section pianists in the world – and he gave it up. He did it graciously, without unseemly fuss, but gradually the piano became less and less prominent until, towards the end of his career, he seems to have abandoned playing entirely.

The process started in 1939, when the King Cole Trio was appearing at Kelly's Stables in New York City. The club's manager asked Nat if he would sing a few numbers during the set, to add a bit of variety. After some hesitation he agreed, and so began the first stage of Nat King Cole's vocal career.

Almost from that moment, the King Cole Trio set a style which became immensely popular – light, lively vocals set to a soft, swinging beat. inconsequential little pieces like *The Frim-Fram Sauce* and *Straighten Up And Fly Right* formed the bulk of its reper-

toire, with occasional ballads such as *'Tis Autumn* and *Gee, Baby, Ain't I Good To You?* Nat's warm voice was instantly recognizable and accounted for the group's huge following but, because the trio had started as an instrumental group, there was as much emphasis on playing as on singing. Not only was Nat himself a renowned pianist; the guitarist, Oscar Moore, was also a leading player. He too had won awards from jazz magazines and was strongly featured, as was bassist Wesley Prince.

As long as Nat was sitting at the piano in the midst of the group, whispering confidences into the microphone, this delicate balance was maintained. It was when strings began to be added for recordings that the balance started to break down. Ballads gradually supplanted rhythm numbers, Nat's voice grew more prominent, and soon his evolution into a solo singer became inevitable. And it must be admitted that his warm, enfolding tones sounded just right with a cushion of violins. With songs like *Unforgettable* and *Nature Boy*, Nat Cole became the first black romantic singer to achieve a popularity comparable with that of

Sinatra and Crosby. The curious thing about it, though, is that there is very little obvious jazz influence in his later ballad style. The phrasing and rhythmic poise are, naturally, impeccable, but he almost never displaces an accent or varies a note of the melody. All the emphasis is placed on the beauty of his voice. And it is beautiful – resonant, lustrous and melting.

You can't blame a man for taking advantage of an asset like that and making himself into an international star. The obvious comparison in our own time is with George Benson, who has followed a similar path, from admired jazz guitarist to heart-throb balladeer. It was Benson who once countered a mildly critical remark about this process by saying, 'Give me a million dollars to do it, and I'll make you the best jazz album you ever heard.' Nat Cole was never as forthright as that, but his thinking probably ran along similar lines.

By the time of his death, in 1965, Nat King Cole had become an institution – film star, television personality, possessor of gold discs and citations and music industry honours by the dozen. He never gave a hint that he missed the days when he was tipped as the likely successor to Earl Hines and Teddy Wilson.

BUDDY RICH

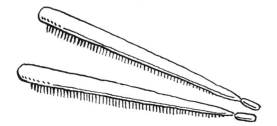

Born into showbusiness and a performer since infancy, Buddy Rich has exploited the idea of the drum solo as a branch of athletics more successfully than anyone else. The Buddy Rich Orchestra is a highly specialized institution, devoted to displaying the leader's virtuosity, and the pleasure of hearing and watching it is the pleasure of witnessing a man doing a difficult thing supremely well. As the years have passed it has also offered the satisfaction of observing the operation of mind over matter. Rich has suffered several serious heart attacks, followed by major surgery, yet comes back every time, looking as manically cheerful as ever.

What all this has to do with art – even an art as loosely buttoned as jazz – is another matter. As a rhythm section player Rich is not subtle and is often dictatorial; drummers with half his technique can create a snappier, lither, more mellow swing. As he slams around the kit, drumsticks a blur of ceaseless movement, the people who applaud loudest tend to be the ones who talk through everything else, and no jazz soloist has been known to compliment him on the quality of his accompaniment.

You will have gathered by now that I remain uncharmed by Buddy Rich, as much for his general manner as for his actual playing. He insists, for instance, that members of his band must turn and watch him when he is going through his solo routines. I don't know why I find this distasteful, but I do. Others don't and there are thousands of them, so maybe I'm wrong.

Dizzy Gillespie

b. 21 October 1917

Dizzy has always been the smiling bebopper. This is in addition, of course, to his phenomenal powers as a trumpeter and improvisor, but the buoyant and cheerful personality has certainly been a great asset. It kept him afloat when his colleagues were struggling against public hostility, armed him against the despair and addiction which blighted so many lives, and continues to sustain him today.

The arrival of bebop, with its complex harmonies, convoluted melodic lines and undanceable tempos, marked the point at which jazz parted company with simple entertainment. Gillespie's genial eccentricity, his beret and goatee beard and manic high spirits, made him a recognizable personality but he was as rigorous a musician as any, and an acknowledged leader of the movement. The big band which he formed in the late forties played music which was not easy, either to play or to listen to, in those early days but Dizzy's clowning sold it. Some of their music sounds pretty ferocious even today, notably pieces like the frantic *Things To Come.*

As the first bebop wave receded, with the death of Charlie Parker, Gillespie's musical approach mellowed somewhat and one could hear quite clearly the elements in his playing which linked him to the great trumpet tradition, back via Roy Eldridge to the great swing trumpeters and, ultimately, to Armstrong. Nevertheless, the immensely long, curling phrases, the fearless pursuit of an idea through remote harmonic territory, the sheer imaginative force burning away behind those ballooning cheeks and owlish spectacles are uniquely his own.

It is impossible to overestimate the influence which Dizzy has had upon the course of jazz: without him the big band tradition would not have turned the corner from the swing era, and the brass/saxes/rhythm line-up might simply have petrified into a nostalgic formula. Without his example trumpet players might never have attempted the fast, crackling phrases which now characterize the instrument in jazz. Without doubt, he was responsible for introducing Latin-American rhythms to modern jazz. Most of all, he has kept everyone's spirits up and proved by example that it is possible to play perfectly serious jazz music without being glum. The bubbling eagerness which he manages still to bring to a night's work is inspiring to any musician.

Ella Fitzgerald

b. 25 April 1918

The books all say 1918, but it has been suggested that Ella was born in 1920. Now, why on earth should a woman make out to be older than she is? Well, according to 'informed sources', it's because she started so young, as vocalist with the Chick Webb orchestra, that Webb was officially breaking the law by employing her full-time. Now that she appears a matronly figure, for all the world like a retired primary school headmistress, it is difficult to imagine Ella Fitzgerald as almost a child star. But once she starts to sing the girlish quality is still there in her voice. Ella's voice is a phenomenon – warm, smooth and apparently ageless.

Arguments about what is a jazz singer and what isn't are suspended where she is concerned, because she is never happier than when she finds herself among jazz musicians. Indeed, when the great drummer Chick Webb died, and she was 21 (or 19), she took the band over and ran it, as leader, for three years. In later years, appearing with *Jazz At The Philharmonic* or guesting with Basie, she always warmed up when it came time to join in with a scat chorus, to be another jazz musician rather than the star vocalist.

In fact, there are two distinct Ellas, the jazz singer described above and the interpreter of classic American song. Ira Gershwin once remarked, 'I never knew how good our songs were until I heard Ella Fitzgerald sing them.' It is certain that her versions, like Sinatra's, have usually turned out to be the definitive ones, and her *Songbook* series is a major contribution to American culture.

Over a space of twelve years, from 1956, she recorded albums of selected songs by Gershwin, Porter, Arlen, Berlin, Ellington, Rodgers and Hart which have remained pretty well permanently in print ever since. Among the items are several which came out as singles and made her voice familiar far beyond the world of jazz – especially Porter's *Every Time We Say Goodbye* and Rodgers and Hart's *Manhattan*.

But these performances are by no means 'straight', if straight means an undeviating reliance on the songsheet. Ella's singing, even in semi-novelty songs like *By Straus*, has the elasticity of time and melody which belongs to the jazz singer. Both sides come together in the perfect duets which she recorded with Louis Armstrong in the mid-fifties. Completely unpretentious – just the two of them and a rhythm section – these sessions produced some of the finest jazz singing ever recorded.

CHARLIE CHRISTIAN

b. 29 July 1919
d. 2 March 1942

The electric guitar is not just an acoustic guitar made louder by amplification. When the Gibson company perfected the electro-magnetic guitar pickup in the late 1930s they invented a new instrument, and it was using one of their very first models, the Gibson ES-150, that Charlie Christian established the electric guitar as a jazz voice. It was in 1940, and he was 21 years old.

He came to New York from Oklahoma City, turned up at a few late night jam sessions, and in no time at all found himself as a featured soloist with Benny Goodman's orchestra, then at the height of its fame. With the clear perception of youth he had grasped the essential fact about the instrument, that it was capable of playing single-line solos, like a saxophone or trumpet, at the same volume and with the same flexibility. Its sound, too, could be made to blend perfectly with wind instruments as an equal partner.

Charlie Christian was also an improvisor of near-genius. His solo lines curled and folded with deceptive ease, displaying an imagination of extraordinary maturity for one of his years. On the few records he made with Lester Young the similarity of the two is uncanny, in both tone and construction. If time could have stood still in 1941, they might have created some of the finest jazz ever recorded. But Christian was already ill with tuberculosis when he joined Goodman, and he died at the age of 23.

His influence has been incalculable. Whenever a jazz guitarist embarks on a single-line solo he is following in Charlie Christian's footsteps, and most of them acknowledge the fact. Just as Lester Young haunts the tenor saxophone, so his ghost haunts the electric guitar.

ART BLAKEY

b. 11 October 1919

Potted biographies of leading American jazz musicians often begin with the words 'Member of Art Blakey's Jazz Messengers . . .' followed by two dates, usually about two years apart. For more than thirty years Blakey has been leading this ever-changing group, grinning delightedly behind the drums as yet another of his young discoveries goes through his paces.

Blakey's judgement has always been sound, and frequently inspired. Wayne Shorter, Horace Silver, Keith Jarrett, Wynton Marsalis – these famous names and dozens of others were unknown when they first appeared on Jazz Messengers billings. He doesn't expect them to stay long, and follows their subsequent careers with fatherly pride: 'I just love to see 'em come on, you know?'

No matter how often the personnel changes, there is a fundamental Messengers approach, characterized by exact ensemble playing, knife-edge dynamics and fairly brief solos. There is also Blakey's drumming, authoritative but not dictatorial, a wonder of percussive light and shade.

When occasion demands, he can play so quietly that you feel, rather than hear, the beat. He follows the contours of every solo, raising or lowering the tension, dropping in little punctuations and sidelong comments.

It is this sensitivity which has made him one of the most sought-after drummers in the world. Any session with Blakey in the driving seat has a fair chance of success. The commanding 'snip' of the hi-hat cymbals and the roar of his celebrated press-roll can be guaranteed to keep the rhythm on its toes.

In the early fifties Blakey visited West Africa, where he observed traditional drummers at work and considered ways of incorporating some of their techniques into his own playing. The only obvious result of this was a fascinating work called *Drum Suite*, for two jazz drummers and a number of other percussionists.

At the time of writing Blakey is leading the latest Messengers group, containing the superb young trumpeter Terence Blanchard. His music has never been more popular and he has never looked happier.

Charlie Parker

b. 29 August 1920

d. 12 March 1955

In the words of his biographer, Ross Russell, Charlie Parker was the 'last apprentice' to emerge from the Kansas City jam sessions of the thirties. Throughout his career he built his improvisations on the same 12-bar and 32-bar patterns that he had mastered as a teenager – but he found far more complex shapes in the old blues and ballads than his mentors had ever dreamed possible.

To listen to Charlie Parker playing a simple blues is to hear a musical mind working on several tasks at once, at impossible speed. Firstly there are the notes, then their rhythmic placement, and finally the shape of the whole solo.

Parker gave the impression of an ever-changing series of possibilities. A harmony could be resolved this way or that; a chromatic shift could lead the melody through a fascinating detour to land finally in the appointed place. While doing this he would deploy phrases and accents in such a way that the inattentive listener might be tricked into thinking that he had missed a beat until, several bars later, the dropped stitch would be picked up casually and the whole thing would come into line again. He could do this for several choruses at a time, never quite tying up the loose ends until the final note.

Even more amazing was that he could do all this when stoned to the eyeballs on gin or even heroin. During the famous recording of *Loverman* made at the 1946 session he collapsed and had to be taken to hospital. He barely gets through the number, but even here his strategy is immaculate, the phrasing typically wily and off-centre. Charlie Parker was not a genius *because* of his weaknesses, but *in spite* of them.

Parker (known to jazz lovers as 'Bird') was the leading figure of the bebop school, the movement which, in the early forties, decisively broke the connection between jazz and popular entertainment. Some regarded this as a great liberation, others saw it as the beginning of hard times, in which jazz would gradually be pushed towards the margins and become an art for insiders, ripe for the attention of theorists and the preserve of the avant-garde. As far as Parker himself was concerned, the first is true. The second never quite happened, but jazz became a far more self-conscious affair from his time onwards.

Thelonious MONK

b. 10 October 1920

d. 17 February 1982

His parents can't have known it at the time, but they gave Thelonious Sphere Monk a name which was to match his music to perfection; the sound of the one instantly calls the other to mind. In the course of his life his public reputation went through three distinct phases – from harmless lunatic to fashionable eccentric artist to revered elder statesman. It is entirely probable that Monk himself noticed none of this, except for the fact that he was working more regularly during the last two periods, and that the pianos were in tune.

He arrived on the scene with the bebop movement of the forties and, in a sense, he was the most thoroughgoing bebopper of them all. He took the harmonic innovations of Bud Powell and Charlie Parker and followed them through with a kind of manic persistence. The result was dauntingly spare and angular. Even for insiders it proved a bit much, and throughout the forties and early fifties Monk worked little and recorded less. But the music he did manage to record in those early days, often in cheap studios and under dreadful conditions, includes some of his very best. His first (1947) version of *Round Midnight*, for instance, is magnificent. This piece has become established now as a minor standard and, because it has a slow tempo, most people play it as a soft, romantic ballad. But listen to Monk's original performance and you will hear it as he heard it – sombre, menacing, full of flitting shadows and midnight fears.

Monk was a true jazz composer, very similar in his methods to Jelly Roll Morton. He worked inside the band, at the piano, shaping and guiding the music but actually writing very little. For this reason he liked to work with musicians whose playing was familiar to him, such as the trumpeter Ray Copeland and saxophonist Charlie Rouse.

As for his celebrated eccentricities, which were supposed to bear out the popular view of his music, they didn't amount to much really. He had a liking for hats, of which he possessed a large collection – Russian fur, Chinese coolie, skull cap etc. He kept an inflexible personal rule never to change hats in the course of a day; whichever hat he stepped out in, that was that day's hat. This foible aside, his oddities were really only the defences of a stubbornly private man. He refused to give press interviews or to take part in any public activity other than the performance of his music. The only person in whom he would confide was his wife, Nellie, who always travelled with him. His life was much like his music: self-enclosed and organized on principles of his own devising.

DAVE BRUBECK

b. 6 December 1920

It is hard now to see what all the fuss was about, but in the late fifties the Dave Brubeck Quartet was enormously popular. Brubeck's picture appeared on the cover of *Time* magazine, and the quartet's record of *Take Five* actually got into the pop singles charts in 1961.

Their biggest audience was in American colleges, where they appealed to young people who considered rock to be beneath their notice. Brubeck's studious manner, his copious references to Milhaud and Hindemith in press interviews, his little lectures at concerts on how very complicated and demanding the next number was going to be, his quotations from Bach, the galloping pomposity of his piano solos – all these combined to make him irresistibly attractive to the kind of students who, ten years before, would have been falling for the same line from Stan Kenton.

Brubeck had studied with Milhaud but, apart from a few years in late adolescence, had no real experience as a jazz musician, certainly not enough to amount to an apprenticeship. He was always the leader of every band he played in, and so had never had the self-indulgence knocked out of his playing. The result was a grotesque mixture of fiddling intricacy and hysterical crashing about. It almost never swung, and the rare occasions when it did were the ones when Brubeck was unwontedly subdued. His fascination with irregular time signatures, such as 5/4 and 7/4, made good jazz phrasing practically impossible in any case.

Brubeck's popularity vanished almost overnight, when college kids suddenly decided that it was all right to like rock. (A few years later they were fans of Cream and Deep Purple.) Strangely enough, he does not seem to have attracted a nostalgia following, which usually happens about 25 years after the original peak.

PAUL DESMOND

b. 25 November 1924

d. 30 May 1977

Paul Desmond, the quartet's alto saxophonist, was a much better jazz player than Brubeck himself. His delicate, piping sound and cool phrasing were invariably charming. Whenever he played in a different context — for instance on his 1959 album with guitarist Jim Hall — he proved what an admirably original musician he was.

Desmond died in 1977, just as he was beginning to be regarded as an independent artist.

ERROLL GARNER

b. 15 June 1921
d. 2 January 1977

Next to Basie, Erroll Garner had the most immediately identifiable piano style in jazz. But Basie has been imitated endlessly, and little bits of him turn up in the playing of hundreds of pianists. Garner, on the other hand, has had no imitators and remains unique.

Although he recorded with various small bands (including Charlie Parker's quartet) in the forties, Garner's great popularity came as a solo pianist, with discreet bass and drums accompaniment. In this context his extraordinary style worked best, and it changed very little from the first recorded example to his death in 1977. The most noticeable thing about it is the steady, chugging left hand – not Waller-type stride, more like rhythm guitar. Over this he deploys a small but hugely effective collection of phrases and voicings – often placed so far behind the left hand's beat that the two seem likely to part company at any moment. On slow ballads his extraordinary technique allowed him to fill every corner with chords, runs, rolling bass figures and filigree tinkling in the treble. The result is so swooningly over-romantic that I often suspect a flicker of self-parody, which would be in keeping with Garner's cheery good nature.

And he was an attractive character. A tiny, elfin man who needed a telephone directory on top of the piano stool to be comfortable at the keyboard (he used to make great play with a comic insistence that only the Manhattan phone book would do), he could fill a concert hall anywhere in the world and made hundreds – possibly even thousands – of records. One of his favourite stratagems was the keep-'em-guessing introduction. This could go on for several minutes, with great portentous chords, significant pauses and the occasional misleading hint. Then, at the least expected moment, the tune would come tripping out, stepping neatly over the bouncy, four-in-a-bar left hand. It never failed to raise a storm of delighted applause, as you can hear on his most popular album, *Concert By The Sea*.

Curiously enough, Garner never learned to read music and was, indeed, entirely self-taught. However, along with a miraculous musical ear he also had the advantage of being completely ambidextrous. He seems to have been unconcerned about technical difficulties and even recorded on one occasion with a broken finger in a splint. As a composer he is best known for his ballad *Misty*, but he also composed and recorded a number of attractive impressionistic pieces, such as *Turquoise, Pastel* and *Impressions*.

Erroll Garner died a fairly rich man. This is a tribute partly to his expert and intelligent manager, Martha Glaser, but most of all to the broad appeal of his music. There are thousands of people who own a couple of Erroll Garner records who would never describe themselves as real jazz fans.

CHARLIE MINGUS

Charles Mingus was a truculent, opinionated, brilliant man. Although he had, by sheer willpower, made himself into a virtuoso of the double bass at an absurdly early age, Mingus could never settle into the life of a jobbing musical craftsman. From the early fifties, with his reputation as an instrumentalist assured, he began to experiment with composition or, rather, creative band-leading, which was his true metier.

Nothing about Charles Mingus was tidy. A shambling, bow-legged figure, he exhorted and bullied his sidemen through wild, tortuous themes which they complained were unplayable. And then, just when a piece was achieving some kind of cohesion, he would change his mind, tear it all to pieces and start again. Yet this maddening wilfulness produced works which, once they were recorded, sounded authoritative and inevitable.

His explosive personality manifested itself in many ways. At a time when jazz musicians still regarded themselves primarily as entertainers, albeit of a special kind, Mingus produced pieces like *Fables Of Faubus*, in which he mocked the racist governor of Arkansas with derisive whoops and yells. He was in the habit of lecturing inattentive audiences and making life impossible for promoters and managers.

Yet he was also a master of the most delicate and poignant impressionism, a trait which he shared with the one man he unreservedly admired – Duke Ellington. The album *Tijuana Moods* is a wonderfully sustained evocation of the life of a Mexican border town. He would have sneered at the pop marketing term 'concept album', but *Tijuana Moods* is perhaps the finest example of this genre ever recorded.

Even when he came to write his autobiography, *Beneath The Underdog*, he did it the hard way, telling his story in the third person, through the eyes of others.

In the late sixties it seemed that he had burned himself out. He retired from music, living on New York's Lower East Side in dire poverty. But he returned to make several more splendid albums until, in 1978, he suffered an illness which left him completely paralyzed. The last report before his death in the following year was of him bawling further impossible demands at his musicians from a wheelchair.

MILT JACKSON

b. 1 January 1923

On the face of it, the vibraphone is an unlikely instrument for jazz, yet ever since Hampton recorded his first solo with Armstrong in 1930 there has been a great vibraphone player in each generation. Milt Jackson, known as 'Bags', is the one from the generation of Parker and Gillespie. He evolved a style which was universally imitated until the advent of Gary Burton, and remains a vastly admired jazz musician. A wonderfully elegant improvisor, he has always been particularly good with the blues. There is a clarity and directness in his style and he produces a rippling, crystalline sound. Milt Jackson makes much use of the instrument's vibrator-fans, and this imparts an attractive warmth to his tone.

For more than twenty years Bags was a member of the Modern Jazz Quartet, or MJQ as it is usually called. This group grew out of the first Dizzy Gillespie big band, being, in fact, originally the band's rhythm section plus Jackson, who was a featured soloist. Their first recordings went under the name of the Milt Jackson Quartet (also MJQ), but the pianist John Lewis took an increasingly prominent role until it was virtually his outfit.

Lewis, a classically trained musician, had long been interested in the idea of introducing more extended forms into jazz, and the MJQ was the ideal medium for his work. Gradually his shapely, semi-classical pieces became typical of the MJQ's repertoire, with Bags unleashed from time to time on the blues or standard. This generated enormous tensions among the musicians, but it was not until 1974 that Jackson finally left amid a shower of recriminations. Ten years later the quartet reformed, with old quarrels apparently forgotten and large cheques in the offing.

Lewis is a very talented composer and the music he wrote for the quartet is always charming and sometimes more than that, notably his score for the film *Sait-On Jamais*, set in Venice, and such pieces as *The Golden Striker, Fontessa* and *Django*. The light tonal quality produced by vibraphone, piano, bass and drums suits his fastidious imagination perfectly.

Also, the tension between Lewis and Jackson did at least ensure there always had to be some concession to Bags, in the form of swinging passages in which he could stretch out. This maintained a precarious balance between formality and improvisation which kept the music from becoming too bland.

Bags continues to tour as a featured soloist with concert packages, playing as delightfully as ever. Best among his recent records is a superb 1983 duet album with Oscar Peterson.

Buddy De Franco

When Boniface Ferdinand Leonardo De Franco – Buddy for short – embarked on his career as a jazz clarinettist in 1939 he was a late entry in a crowded field. Ten years later, with his technique perfected and style fully formed, he found himself in a minority of one.

Jazz had undergone a revolution and the clarinet, strongly associated with the old guard of Benny Goodman and Artie Shaw, had been dropped like a hot brick. Its sound just didn't seem to fit into the revised scheme of things, and it was much harder to play the new, highly chromatic style on the clarinet than on the saxophone.

Nevertheless, perched in lonely eminence and with no rivals to stimulate him, De Franco played on. His dexterity seemed superhuman and he expressed an endless flow of ideas with a tone like polished ice, as he does to this day. No matter how fast the tempo, he constructs long and immensely complicated lines as though he had all the time in the world. The clarinet has an effective range of some three and a half octaves and De Franco regularly pursues variations on a single phrase from one end to the other, sometimes tricking the ear with tiny ambiguities of rhythm or harmony in the process.

If a musician can be judged by the company he keeps, then De Franco is one of the greats. He has worked with Basie, Art Tatum, Oscar Peterson, Art Blakey and dozens of others. Beginning in 1947, he collected 19 consecutive 'Down Beat' awards but, even so, he gave up his career as a jazz soloist in 1966 to front the 'official' Glen Miller orchestra for eight years.

Since his return in 1974 he has been touring and recording extensively. Some of his finest recent recordings are of live performances in Argentina and Great Britain.

J. J. Johnson

b. 22 January 1924

New styles demand new techniques, and bebop provided an enormous challenge to any instrumentalist. For the trombone it seemed next to impossible; the quick-fire delivery of Parker and Gillespie might have been designed purposely to defeat the trombone slide. J. J. Johnson was the man who proved it could be done. As a member of Charlie Parker's recording quintet in 1947 he moved with unprecedented agility.

To do it he had to abandon much of the traditional trombone vocabulary, the smears and rips, the muted effects and ripe vibrato. The result was hard-edged and angular, crisp and rather cold in tone, but it worked. And, having set the standard, he had the dubious satisfaction of having a whole generation emulating him and even equalling his mercurial phrasing.

In the fifties he formed a quintet with another trombonist, Kai Winding, called 'Jay and Kai', and together they produced a beautiful blend of tones. In one piece, *Don't Argue*, they chased each other like a couple of kittens, moving with amazing ease through difficult chromatic harmonies.

For a while after that J. J. left the music business, but he returned a few years ago, and when last heard was playing as well as ever.

Sarah Vaughan

b. 27 March 1924

Nobody ever conveyed a physical delight in the very act of singing more vividly than the young Sarah Vaughan. She was the vocalist of the Parker-Gillespie generation, the first to be able to handle the very un-vocal intervals and difficult chromatic shifts which their music demanded. Her entry into the music business had been as relief pianist with the Earl Hines orchestra in 1943, and this harmonic knowledge no doubt helped. Whatever the case, to hear Sarah in her early twenties lifting a song away from its melody line and soaring effortlessly through a barrage of augmented ninths and flattened fifths is one of the great thrills of jazz.

I would not say that her powers are in any way diminished today but, after 40-odd years, that sense of discovery is rarely present. Instead there is a singer with an enormous range – down into the baritone register and up pretty well to where she could reach as a teenager.

At times she still takes terrifying risks – piling into four scat choruses without bothering to sing the tune first, reversing the beat, skating on very thin harmonic ice. But there are certain expectations of female singers who use the kind of repertoire that she uses:

they are expected to be interpreters of songs. Sarah has never been particularly interested in the words of the tunes she sings; as a child of the bebop generation her instinct is to dig straight down into the infra-structure and start rebuilding.

This misapprehension has led, over the years, to some pretty bizarre results, of which the oddest is probably her version of *Send In The Clowns*. If ever a song was unsuited to a singer like Sarah Vaughan, this must be it – fragile little melody, no real harmonic development and all the interest concentrated in the words. I have heard Sarah smash it to rubble on many occasions and wondered why she bothered; the answer is that it is probably the most popular item in her repertoire. That and *Passing Strangers*, which she recorded as a duet with Billy Eckstine many years ago and from which neither of them can now escape.

And yet I have heard her sit down at the piano in the middle of a concert and, almost absent-mindedly, pick her way through *Once In A While* with the gazelle-like sure-footedness of her youth. It's still all there, in working order, and when she chooses to turn it on the effect is wonderful.

Bud Powell

Listen to any of the great bebop pianists – Al Haig, Duke Jordan, George Wallington – and then listen to Bud Powell. With none of the others can you quite forget the thirty-odd years between you and them. Only Bud's music is as startling now as it was then. At his best he could produce an endless flow of ideas, constantly changing the rhythmic patterns of his line while subjecting the basic harmony to a bewildering series of alterations. There are moments on some of his best records when the sheer impetus of his playing leaves you gasping. Apart from Parker, there's nobody who thinks quicker or takes more chances, and in a piece like *Bud's Bubble*, recorded in 1947, the gambles all come off.

It is possible to write down a chorus of Bud's most tempestuous playing, subject it to rigorous analysis and justify every single note. The mind capable of such feats must have been quite extraordinary.

Unfortunately, the mind of Bud Powell was not a very stable article. He was plagued by mental illness for most of his life and spent long periods in hospital. As he got older his affliction became worse, and even leaving the United States and the pressures of life in New York to take up residence in France only relieved the situation for a while.

He called one of his compositions *The Glass Enclosure*, and the title seems to sum up his state of mind. It was as though he were separated from the world by an invisible cage. He would go for days without speaking to a soul, and on the bandstand he would often sit staring blankly ahead of him, suddenly lift his hands to the keyboard and begin to play without telling his accompanists what he was going to do.

To those of us who heard him in person at this period in his life, a Bud Powell set could be rather an unnerving experience. Sometimes, certainly, he would play with a trace of his earlier brilliance, but often he lacked the co-ordination to bring his ideas off. The extraordinary thing was that, underneath it all, you could almost sense the ideas fighting to get out.

MAX ROACH

b. 10 January 1925

Max Roach was *the* bebop drummer. He plays on practically all Charlie Parker's classic recordings between 1946 and 1948 and is perhaps the most influential drummer in the whole of modern jazz.

It was Roach who made the decisive move of shifting the job of time-keeping from the hi-hat or snare drum to the top cymbal. This apparently tiny change altered the whole emphasis of jazz rhythm; it gave the drums a punctuating, commenting role for the first time and threw the task of marking the beat largely on to the bass.

The quintet which he co-led with the trumpeter Clifford Brown in the mid-fifties remains one of the classic jazz groups, and its records have been reissued constantly.

After Brown's death, Max Roach became increasingly involved in the US civil rights movement and much of his work acquired a propagandist tinge, with titles such as *We Insist!* and *Tears For Johannesburg*. The album *Percussion Bitter Sweet* is a particularly good one from this period.

A modest, serious man, Roach has done a great deal of teaching in recent years, and also formed an all-percussion group, called M'Boom, which owes as much to the African drum tradition as it does to jazz.

b. 6 March 1925

d. 15 June 1968

Probably the most imitated jazz guitarist after Charlie Christian, Wes was a late starter. He was 34 when he left his native Indianapolis to join his brothers Monk (a bassist) and Buddy (a pianist) in the group, the Mastersounds. Once heard, however, his extraordinary fluency and revolutionary self-developed technique carried him to the top of every jazz magazine poll in America within a couple of years.

The new and distinctive sound which he produced was made possible by discarding the plectrum and plucking the strings with his thumb. In place of the hard-edged, highly defined effect which all post-Christian players had sought to perfect, Wes brought a warm bloom to the tone of the electric guitar. He had also developed a technique for playing fast passages in octaves – something never previously attempted. Both these elements have now been absorbed and become standard practice among jazz guitarists.

Technique aside, Wes Montgomery was in any case a superb jazz musician, especially when it came to playing the blues. The albums of his early career, on the Riverside label, are full of examples of his mastery of simple structures and his immense ingenuity in exploiting them. Later records, for Verve, are a disappointment. Overproduced and formula-ridden, they provide a typical example of what happens when big corporations try to smarten jazz up.

No doubt Wes Montgomery would soon have gone back to more congenial surroundings, but he died at the age of 43.

WES MONTGOMERY

OSCAR

PETERSON

To have pursued a well ordered career, lived a thoroughly respectable life and, at the age of sixty, to be able to look back with portly affability on a history of achievement and personal satisfaction – these things do not make one interesting to the media. Since this has been the pattern of Oscar Peterson's life it is not surprising that very little has actually been written about him. Yet he is one of the best known jazz musicians ever, a television face and tireless traveller.

He is Canadian by birth, and still retains the round Canadian vowels in his speech, even though he left his native Montreal in 1949. His entire career has been managed by one man, the impresario Norman Granz, founder of Jazz At The Philharmonic and owner of the Pablo record label. As a result, Peterson is one of the most prolific recording artists in jazz history, as both soloist and accompanist. Because of his great technical virtuosity, Peterson's self-effacing talent in accompanying others has tended to be overlooked. But listen to his work on the *Ella And Louis* albums and behind Sonny Stitt or Ben Webster and you will hear some extraordinarily sensitive and intelligent backing piano.

However, it is as a soloist that he first made his name, and his superb, effortless technique has never been known to let him down. The great thing about his playing is

b. 15 August 1925

that, with all that power at his disposal, he is rarely if ever glib or facile; everything is considered and carefully shaped.

At one time he also made a few albums as a singer, rather after the style of Nat King Cole, and this gave rise to the only really colourful story ever told about Oscar Peterson. Apparently, when Nat heard the records he said to Oscar, 'I'll make a deal with you. I promise never to play the piano in public again if you promise not to sing.' Whatever the truth of this, it is certain that Cole never again played the piano on record and Peterson never recorded another vocal during Cole's lifetime.

The name and face of Oscar Peterson are known well beyond the jazz world, so much so that a recent television advertisement for electric pianos simply showed him playing one, without need to mention who he was. Similarly, his name alone will draw capacity audiences to concert halls around the world, many of whose members would never think of attending a show by any other jazz musician.

John Haley Sims couldn't remember exactly where or when he had acquired his famous nickname, 'Zoot'. Some time back in the early forties, he supposed, when he was a teenage bandsman, and zoot suits were all the rage.

He was not just a superb tenor saxophonist, but one of the unmistakable jazz voices. With his blithe, open phrasing and feather-edged tone you could spot him instantly, however unlikely the company. And he did turn up in some pretty unexpected places.

But Zoot's artistry amounted to more than a journeyman's bag of tricks. Like most tenor saxophonists of his generation, he was a follower of Lester Young, whose advice to young musicians was simply, 'Tell your story.' In Zoot's playing there was always a clear thread of narrative, a musical discourse which, like all good stories, kept you guessing what would happen next. His fluency was astounding, yet so conversational in tone that he made everything he did sound easy.

He first came to the notice of the jazz public in 1947, as a member of Woody Herman's orchestra. At the time he was virtually indistinguishable from the legion of Lester Young disciples, of whom Getz was the most celebrated. But Zoot's subsequent career is probably unique, in that he continued developing for almost four decades. One can take a record from any point in his life and, without looking at the date, place it to within a year or two. Generally speaking, the later it is, the better.

In his last ten years he recorded a string of albums for the Pablo label which show him at his peak – mellow and poised, at once delicate and robust. He had reached that rare stage of mastery at which he could merely play the tune and make it sound as though he had just invented it. And the tunes he chose to play constituted a guided tour of the byways of American song – *I Hear A Rhapsody, On The Alamo, Dream Dancing, Emily*. Along with everything else, Zoot was a guardian of the repertoire.

ZOOT SIMS

b. 29 October 1925
d. 22 March 1985

MILES

b. 25 May 1926

Nobody listening to Miles Davis in his first few years as a trumpet player would ever have tipped him as a future jazz superstar. His first recordings with Charlie Parker, in 1945, show him to have been a competent player, but by no means a virtuoso, with an unusual dry tone. Over the next couple of years hints of the future Miles began to peep out, usually in slow ballads – curious and laconic little turns of phrase.

But what Miles Davis did have was enormous self-confidence. The sound of his trumpet may be shy and gentle, but the man himself seems always to have been at the centre of whatever was happening, usually in the leading role. Take, for instance, the celebrated nine-piece band of 1948–9, which established new standards in jazz orchestration. The band appeared and recorded under Miles's name, although it was really a joint project along with Gil Evans, Gerry Mulligan and others. His fragile tone, so different from the conventional lead trumpet sound, gives subtle colour to the whole ensemble. And the willpower that took him, as a very young and technically unremarkable player, to the centre of jazz activity, also enabled him to beat a brief spell of heroin addiction.

The rise of Miles Davis to the level of glamorous culture hero, and also to real importance as a jazz musician, came in 1955, when he appeared at the Newport Jazz Festival and completely stopped the show. Although he affected surprise and indifference ('I always play like that'), Miles busily set about forming a quartet with which to capitalize on this new popularity. The band, with John Coltrane on tenor saxophone and drummer Philly Joe Jones, became one of the classic groups in jazz. In particular, it focused the poignant, lost qual-

DAVIS

ity in Miles's style, especially when playing muted.

This sound, both in the quintet and accompanied by sumptuous orchestrations by Gil Evans, was enormously attractive, and quickly became the background music to fashionable life in New York, London and Paris. The portraits of Miles on the record sleeves depicted him always as the epitome of chic, casually but faultlessly dressed and coolly watchful.

A less intelligent man would have hung on to this style for as long as possible, but Miles began a series of bewildering changes, first to the 'modal' jazz of *Kind Of Blue*, then, after the departure of Coltrane, to a drier, more glancing and angular music. The big change, though, came with the album *In A Silent Way* – the beginning of Miles Davis as leader of the jazz-rock movement. This was in 1969, when you couldn't *give* jazz away to most young people. Yet, within a couple of years, Miles was packing rock venues, such as Fillmore West and the Rainbow, with audiences half his age.

Now, at the age of 60, and following a long illness, he's back again, playing in a curiously detached manner, as though contemplating the next move.

JOHN COLTRANE

b. 23 September 1926

d. 17 July 1967

Although he died in 1967, the influence of John Coltrane is still powerfully at work in jazz today. It is practically impossible to find a tenor saxophone player below the age of about 35 who does not to some extent echo his sound and approach.

He had been a working musician since the late forties, but Coltrane seemed suddenly to arrive when he joined the Miles Davis Quintet in 1955. He was greeted first with costernation. His metallic, unyielding tone and angular phrasing struck many listeners as being deliberately ugly, but there was also a massive authority about his musical presence which could not be denied. It was during Coltrane's time with the quintet that Miles Davis made one of those inspired changes of direction for which he is well known. In this case the move was in the direction of modal playing – improvising on scales rather than on sequences of chords. This concept suited Coltrane perfectly, and set his musical course for the rest of his life.

Whereas a chord sequence, such as is found underlying standard songs, moves purposefully through a series of resolutions to a conclusion, a mode can go on for ever because it contains no tension and therefore does not demand to be resolved. Harmonic resolution is a fairly recent product of Western European culture and enacts in music the idea of progress and material achievement. Modes, on the other hand, like Indian ragas, are characteristic of more static and contemplative societies. John Coltrane was a naturally thoughtful person, increasingly occupied in spiritual meditation. From about 1959, when he formed his first quartet, until the end of his life his music echoes this cast of mind.

Like the Armstrong Hot Fives or the Miles Davis Quintets, the quartet's records form one of the great classic jazz series. From the delicate stillness of *Naima* (1959) to the hugely impressive devotional work *A Love Supreme* (1965), they form a coherent statement in a dialect of the jazz language which Coltrane had hammered out for his own purposes. The rhythm section sets up a rolling sea of sound, turbulent but hypnotic, through which the saxophone ploughs and bobs. Coltrane had by this time added the soprano saxophone to his customary tenor, and its sharp, plaintive cry is particularly effective.

I find the work of his last couple of years, after *A Love Supreme*, completely incomprehensible, which is not to say that it is meaningless. Others have certainly found much delight in it.

RAY BROWN

b. 13 October 1926

To use a well worn expression, Ray Brown wrote the book on bass playing, only in his case there really is a book. It's called the 'Ray Brown Bass Method', and there are few serious bass players in jazz who don't possess a copy.

Ever since he joined Dizzy Gillespie, at the age of 19, Raymond Matthews Brown has been revered for his tone, his time and, most of all, for his lines. The bass is the instrument on which the jazz rhythm section is built, and the line that it lays down must be firm, melodic and, above all, harmonically clear. In this respect Ray Brown lifted the standard of rhythm section playing by several hundred per cent. In 1946 he recorded a virtuoso feature number, *One Bass Hit*, with Dizzy's first big band, which also set new standards for sheer technique.

There was never any doubt that Ray Brown was one of the great jazz musicians.

For more than forty years he has been at the centre (or, more correctly, at the root) of jazz activity – particularly with the Oscar Peterson Trio, Jazz At The Philharmonic and literally hundreds of superb recording sessions. He also became Quincy Jones's business manager and worked on developing the first really effective amplifier for the double bass.

For a while his business activities kept him away from regular playing, but in the 1970s he was back full time, touring with the LA Four and busy in the recording studios once more.

STAN GETZ

Strictly speaking, the Brothers were the four young saxophonists featured on Woody Herman's 1947 recording *Four Brothers*, but the Brotherhood was really a whole generation of white tenor saxophone players, born in the mid-twenties, who drew their inspiration from Lester Young. Of the original four – Herbie Steward, Stan Getz, Zoot Sims, Serge Chaloff – it was Getz who rose highest and fastest and who was, for a time, the most imitated tenor player in the world.

The fashion at the beginning of the fifties was for 'cool' sounds, unemotional, graceful, spare. Getz, his high, piping tone and uninflected phrasing, caught the hip ear with a solo on Herman's *Early Autumn* in 1948, exactly the right moment, and he was soon a name on his own account. The records he made during this first period are mainly pale, watercolour versions of standard tunes. Without exception they are charming, although sometimes so reticent that he seems to be talking to himself. Getz was then in his very early twenties and these performances had a profound effect upon young players around the world. Indeed, on film soundtracks of the time an impression of youth and modernity is often conveyed with the help of a vaguely Getzian saxophone sighing away in the background.

As a leader of fashion Getz was soon displaced, but that's when some quite extraordinary developments in his tone and attack started to take place. There was an album in 1957, with the trombonist J. J. Johnson, which found him adopting a new, bustling approach and, shortly afterwards, a quartet record, *The Steamer*, where he sounds as though he's playing inside a tea-cosy. But gradually a lustrous sound began to emerge with a kind of glow at the centre. It was unlike anything the tenor saxophone had hitherto produced – and that's saying a lot, because no instrument has more potential tonal variety.

From this point, in the late fifties, Getz developed his unique practice of using shading, dynamics and variations in tone to make his point. The album *Focus*, on which he plays compositions by Eddie Sauter, accompanied by a small string orchestra, grasps this essentially dramatic side of Getz's talent and exploits it to the full.

Getz appeals to an audience far beyond the jazz world. In the early sixties his series of albums with leading Brazilian musicians was largely responsible for the *bossa nova* craze, and brought him a couple of hit records. (He used to announce *Desafinado* as 'the tune that's putting my kids through college'.) Some of his very best playing is to be heard on *Jazz Samba* and *Getz and Gilberto*, the two most popular bossa nova albums.

As a spotter and encourager of new talent Getz is second only to Art Blakey. Through the sixties and seventies he led a series of small bands, made up of young and promising players. They always played some material written by them and Getz adopted his own playing to their ideas. In the last few years, however, he has gone back to playing the material of the forties and fifties, and working with musicians of his own generation once more. The results so far have been magnificent.

From the crew-cut college boy of the early fifties to the bearded Old Testament prophet of thirty years later, Gerry Mulligan has changed dramatically in appearance but scarcely at all in his playing. He has, it is true, added the soprano saxophone to his customary baritone, but it is as a baritone player that Mulligan will always be most celebrated. He brought a new agility to this sturdy bottom voice of the saxophone section, causing it to speak in light and airy tones.

In 1952 Mulligan formed a quartet which was considered revolutionary at the time, because it did not contain a piano or other chord-playing instrument. The group consisted of Mulligan on baritone, Chet Baker on trumpet, bassist Carson Smith and drummer Chico Hamilton and, despite the fuss about its unconventional instrumentation, it quickly became all the rage. In Britain record companies were caught off-guard and for some months imported copies and illegal dubbings of the Mulligan quartet's first ten-inch LP were changing hands at black market prices. It is easy to see why the group was such an instant success; cool and fluent, with witty arrangements and tuneful, optimistic-sounding solos, the Gerry Mulligan Quartet's sound remains one of the most charming in the whole of jazz. On that first album the Mulligan compositions *Walking Shoes* and *Nights At The Turntable* are typical of the approach.

Along with his virtuosity on the baritone saxophone, Mulligan is also a splendid orchestrator. He was one of the moving spirits behind the Miles Davis band of the late forties, and continued to develop his interest in medium-sized ensembles with a band called the Tentette, which recorded one album for Capitol in 1954.

Although he has never since achieved quite the pristine sparkle of those early years, Mulligan has always made enjoyable and well constructed music. His Concert Band of the sixties was especially tasty, featuring such soloists as Zoot Sims and Clark Terry. One refreshing aspect of Gerry Mulligan is his complete lack of self-importance, an attribute which goes well with a whimsical sense of humour. One of his pieces bears the very Mulliganesque title *Butterfly With Hiccups*.

For an artist like Gerry Mulligan – accomplished, witty, readily comprehensible but full of subtlety – the sixties and seventies were not the most sympathetic of times. However, he is now back in the limelight, leading an occasional big band playing his compositions and touring as a soloist.

b. 6 April 1927

GERRY MULLIGAN

E L V I N

Ever since his days as drummer with the classic John Coltrane Quartet, Elvin Jones has been renowned for his intricate rhythms and a beat which sounds like Atlantic rollers – shifting, tumbling but inevitable. He is so relaxed that he seems to be playing in slow motion, but his constructions are full of surprise and wit.

Since leaving Coltrane he has led a series of bands of his own – all carefully chosen to produce a result as unlike an imitation of Coltrane's group as possible. Most drumming bandleaders assert their position by playing at deafening volume all the time but Jones, a fit, powerfully built man, relies upon subtlety rather than muscle.

For some reason, he calls his present band the Rhythm Machine, although anything less mechanical it is difficult to imagine. Before each performance Elvin's diminutive Japanese wife Keiko comes on stage and tunes the drum kit – a delicate job which no other serious percussionist has been known to delegate to anyone.

JONES

BILL EVANS

b. 16 August 1929

d. 15 September 1980

The amount of enjoyment you get from the piano music of Bill Evans depends on the acuteness of your ear. You don't have to know anything about music, but you do need to be able to hear more than simply the tune. Evans's great strength lay in the harmonic shading which he could impart to any song – even the theme tune from Walt Disney's *Alice In Wonderland*.

He arrived on the jazz scene relatively late in life, at the age of 28, with an album that made very little impression. However, Miles Davis heard it, and in 1958 Evans joined the Miles Davis Quintet, the best possible time for a player of his quiet subtlety. This was the moment when Miles was working on his modal compositions, and the first that most people heard of Bill Evans was on the immensely successful album *Kind Of Blue*. Although he stayed with the band for less than nine months, his reputation was made.

It was after leaving Miles that he formed the trio which was to be his setting for the rest of his life. The trio was by no means a one-man show (solo pianist with supporting cast of bass and drums) because it also contained the extraordinary bass player Scott LaFaro. Evans and LaFaro together evolved a method of playing in which the bass was no longer a simple time-keeper; it became a melodic voice, part of the texture. The double bass had never before been as busy as this in a jazz ensemble, and LaFaro's agility was now only possible because he had modified the instrument to allow speed at the expense of volume. This, in turn, was feasible only because the trio played in quiet places, such as concert halls and small jazz rooms, and on account of increasingly efficient bass amplification.

When LaFaro died in a road accident in 1961 Evans simply could not carry on playing, because he had become dependent upon those particular bass lines. It was some months before he re-formed the trio, with Eddie Gomez in LaFaro's place. Gomez played with so light a touch, and

such a high level of amplification, that the bass, in his hands, sounded more like an enormous guitar. The tendency of bass players in subsequent years to follow this pattern has not had entirely pleasing results. It is now very rare to hear the natural, deep tones of the unamplified double bass in jazz.

As for Bill Evans himself, he probably brought jazz piano to its highest possible pitch of chromatic subtlety. He achieved this at the expense of rhythmic impetus and excitement, but the pale, shifting tone colours grow more fascinating the more closely you listen.

SONNY
ROLLINS

Sonny Rollins today is a rather lonely figure in the jazz landscape. In the fifties he was one of the two great tenor saxophonists; the other was John Coltrane, whose use of modes and simplification of harmony turned out to be the more influential. Rollins was content to stick to the blues and the 32-bar song, but what he can do with this basic material is tremendous. Rollins is a strategist, a master of musical hide-and-seek. He begins with a simple tune – something like *Surrey With A Fringe On Top* – and twists and turns, delves deep into the harmonic intricacies and, just when you thought the melody had vanished for ever, up it pops again.

Rollins's roots lie deep in bebop. He played with Parker, Miles Davis, Max Roach and just about every other major figure from the late forties to the sixties. (Incidentally, if you inadvertently play a Rollins album at 45rpm, it sounds remarkably like Charlie Parker.) His best records, so far, are probably the ones made in the mid-fifties, particularly a superb quartet album entitled *Saxophone Colossus*. One of the pieces on it, *Blue Seven*, was taken as the subject of a long analysis by musciologist Gunther Schuller, in which he pointed out how complex Rollins's handling of his material could be. After reading it, Rollins was unable to play for a week, because it made him too conscious of his own thought processes. He gave up reading anything written about him from that moment.

Between 1959 and 1961 Rollins retired from public playing in order to practise and work out new ideas, and it was during this retreat that the story began to circulate that he was to be found playing alone in odd corners of New York City. In fact, he did practise for a while on one of the walkways of the Williamsberg Bridge – not for any mystical reason, but because he didn't want to wake the neighbours' children.

The first album he made on his return was actually entitled *The Bridge*. It wasn't as startlingly different as some had predicted, but in subsequent years the Rollins tone has become an amazingly pliable thing – at one moment thick and fibrous, at the next hollow, and sometimes overlaid with the widest vibrato since Sidney Bechet.

Bob Brookmeyer

b. 19 December 1929

The valve-trombone, as its name suggests, is a hybrid instrument. The same amount of plumbing, arranged in a slightly different way, produces a bass trumpet, and that is very much what the valve trombone sounds like. In jazz it has two noted exponents – Bob Brookmeyer and Ellington's Juan Tizol.

Brookmeyer's playing has a quiet, lyrical quality to it which makes him the perfect second voice in a group. As a result, he spent much of his early career in the shadow of other players, among them Stan Getz, Gerry Mulligan and Clark Terry.

His own style is neatly summed up in the title of one of his albums – *Traditionalism Revisited*. He plays with a ripe, jovial tone and open, melodic phrasing. In every respect he fits perfectly into the white jazz tradition which descends from Bix Beiderbecke, and his style appeals readily to people who have little or no experience of jazz music.

There is, however, another side to Brookmeyer, a melancholy and brooding aspect that surfaces from time to time in his ballad performances. Some splendid examples of this can be found in the album *Bob Brookmeyer and Friends*, featuring Stan Getz and Herbie Hancock.

Although he is best known for his valve trombone playing, Brookmeyer is also a good pianist and arranger.

b. 19 March 1930

ORNETTE

If the term *avant-garde* has any meaning at all in jazz, it started with Ornette Coleman. No-one could say, as people usually do in cases of this kind, that what he played wasn't jazz. It manifestly *was* a kind of jazz and, to the superficial ear, Coleman's themes and his general sound were similar to Parker's. But when you listened closely to the solo line something was disturbingly awry.

Parker would establish a theme, trace solos through the chord sequence and end with the tune again, to tie everything up. Well, Coleman's themes were attractive, in a spiky kind of way, but once Coleman on alto saxophone and his trumpet partner Don Cherry started their excursions, they seemed to skate off on illogical tangents, pursuing a melodic idea with little or no regard for the harmony. Most listeners, not all cloth-eared by any means, simply gave up.

For years before he was accepted and recorded he had been playing this way. He had worked on the rhythm and blues circuit, playing with little bands to audiences who knew exactly what they wanted – and whatever it was, it wasn't free improvisation. Like Parker before him, he seemed driven by a personal demon which he was powerless to control. The titles of his records made a point of telling everyone that here was the musical future, for example *Something Else!, The Shape Of Jazz To Come* and *Change Of The Century*. The extent to which listeners accepted the music depended rather on what they enjoyed about jazz in the first place. Those who were attracted by the self-expression and the iconoclastic, anti-establishment approach welcomed Ornette Coleman warmly; those who liked the swing

and intimacy and wit of jazz couldn't take to him.

This sort of thing has happened before, in both jazz and classical music, but most people have eventually come round. In Coleman's case, however, some kind of crunch seems to have been reached. Almost thirty years later, there are many listeners whose enjoyment of jazz stops dead at Ornette Coleman.

COLEMAN

b. 30 October 1930
d. 26 June 1956

CLIFFORD BROWN

On 21 March 1952, Clifford Brown made his first appearance in the recording studios, as a member of Chris Powell's Blue Flames. Four years and one day later, as an internationally renowned trumpet star, he recorded his last session. His effective recording career was even shorter, lasting less than three years.

It would be absurd to expect much in the way of development in such a short space of time. From first to last the records show a poised, assured musician with formidable technique and a vast store of ideas. Most of all they reveal the energy of youth and a singularly cheerful cast of mind. Brownie, as musicians called him, was also a gifted mathematician and championship-class chess player. Universally liked, becomingly modest and always ready for a little harmless mischief, Clifford Brown was the stuff of which schoolboy heroes are made.

The story has often been told of his exploits during Lionel Hampton's first European tour, when the band were forbidden to play or record outside their normal duties. Naturally, they made a point of doing the exact opposite, and laid down hours of tape for French and Swedish record companies. Clifford was a leading spirit in this – even to the extent of retiring to his hotel room under the eyes of the tour manager, climbing straight out of the window and down the fire escape. As it turns out, these clandestine European recordings make up a sizeable chunk of his output.

When he joined Max Roach, to form the Roach-Brown Quintet, in 1955, his playing seemed to gain even greater confidence and the themes which he wrote for the band (*Joy Spring, Daahoud, George's Dilemma* etc) bring out his essential qualities of melodic fluency and rhythmic cunning.

The bright, crackling tone of Brownie's trumpet, together with his youth and natural ebullience, led him to play far more up-tempo numbers than ballads. Nevertheless, when he did slow down he could produce wonderfully tender performances, and his album with strings is a gem. Most of all, there is a wholeheartedness in everything he played. The full tone, the fizzing attack, the perky little quotations delivered, as it were, with a wink – they all add up to a style which was, by all accounts, the man himself.

The death of Clifford Brown, in a car crash on the Pennsylvania Turnpike in 1956, particularly shocked the jazz world for two reasons. In the first place, Clifford had always been the epitome of health and well-being, and had never had anything to do with drugs. In the second, so many expectations had been piled upon him: Brownie would carry the flame. If he had lived he would still only be in his fifties.

ROLAND KIRK

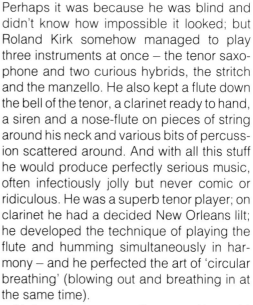

b. 7 August 1936
d. 6 December 1977

Perhaps it was because he was blind and didn't know how impossible it looked; but Roland Kirk somehow managed to play three instruments at once – the tenor saxophone and two curious hybrids, the stritch and the manzello. He also kept a flute down the bell of the tenor, a clarinet ready to hand, a siren and a nose-flute on pieces of string around his neck and various bits of percussion scattered around. And with all this stuff he would produce perfectly serious music, often infectiously jolly but never comic or ridiculous. He was a superb tenor player; on clarinet he had a decided New Orleans lilt; he developed the technique of playing the flute and humming simultaneously in harmony – and he perfected the art of 'circular breathing' (blowing out and breathing in at the same time).

No two sets were ever the same. He would rummage delicately about in his musical junk yard and always come up with something new. There are a few bits of film, and they give some idea, but they're a pale shadow of Kirk's personal presence.

And then, in the mid-seventies, he suffered a stroke. Surely, not even he could overcome being paralyzed down one side? But he did. And he showed me the modifications he had made to his instruments so that they could be played one-handed. 'It's a mechanical problem,' he said, 'and so there must be a mechanical solution.'

Some of the greatest jazz musicians have been very limited in the scope of their talents. It is unlikely, for instance, that Thelonious Monk or Tricky Sam Nanton could ever have done anything but what they actually did. Herbie Hancock, on the other hand, was so vastly gifted from childhood that there must have been a danger of his not settling positively on anything at all. Someone who has played a Mozart concerto with the Chicago Symphony at the age of eleven is faced with an embarrassment of choice. As it turned out, Hancock made the rare and sensible decision to do several things, but to keep them separate.

Thus, he composed one of the very first jazz-funk hits, *Watermelon Man*, played with the Miles Davis Quintet in one of its most fruitful periods, wrote and performed some of the most sophisticated atonal jazz yet recorded (Anthony Williams's *Life Time* and Bobby Hutcherson's *The Omen*) and became a star of electronic disco-funk. Along the way there have been such superb productions as the gentle *Speak Like A Child*, featuring his piano with a small ensemble backing, and the pioneering *Mwandishi*, with its complex rhythms and fascinating electronic tone colours.

There is an old adage to the effect that talent does what it likes, but genius does only what it can – in which case Herbie Hancock is no genius. I doubt whether this worries him unduly.

HERBIE
HANCOCK

b. 12 April 1940

GARY BURTON

b. 23 January 1943

Gary Burton plays the vibraphone as though it were a piano, using four and sometimes six mallets at once. So complete is his command of the instrument that he is able to play completely solo concerts, building wonderful filigree structures of sound. It is almost impossible to make an ugly noise on the vibraphone, but Burton has refined and extended the tonal range of the instrument far beyond tinkling prettiness. He has even devised a method of bending the notes to create a sliding, wailing effect.

He first came to the notice of the jazz public as a member of Stan Getz's quartet in the mid-sixties, but it was with his own band that he perfected the extraordinary virtuosity which marks his work today. The Gary Burton Quartet was one of the few jazz groups to gain a following in the hardest period jazz has ever known – the late sixties. Young, white, fashionable, he found that American college audiences could identify with him, as they could not do with older black musicians. The quartet played music heavily influenced by rock, and even by country music, but this faded after a few years and Burton's style is now entirely his own.

THE INHERITORS

Wynton Marsalis

I have picked out these three young musicians because they are original, technically superb and have attracted a lot of attention recently.

A tremendous fuss has been made about their youth, but people forget how young most of the great jazz musicians were when they first hit town. Charlie Parker was 19 when he joined the Jay McShann Orchestra; Stan Getz was 21, and a seasoned professional, when he recorded *Early Autumn*; Fats Waller was making his living from music at the age of 15. No, the point isn't that they're young. In the case of Jordan and McFerrin it is that they have extended the technical possibilities of jazz, and Wynton Marsalis is an extraordinary artist by any standards.

A genuine child prodigy (he played the Haydn Trumpet Concerto with the New Orleans Symphony at the age of 15), Marsalis was born in 1961, and destined to become a jazz musician. His musician father even named him after Miles Davis's pianist at the time, Wynton Kelly.

With his gifts, he could have picked up any of the loose threads in jazz and spun it out endlessly to universal applause. Significantly, he chose the most daunting – the edgy, abstract style evolved and subsequently abandoned by Miles Davis in the mid-sixties. It demands such powers of concentration, such a ferocious grip on the intricacies of rhythm and line, that it was prudently ignored by one and all for the next 15 years. It was left to Wynton Marsalis to take up this piece of unfinished business, and he does it with that mixture of deliberation and passion that is the mark of the master improvisor. He has also developed into a magnificent player of ballads, and his album *Hot House Flowers* has been hailed as one of the finest trumpet-with-orchestra recordings of all time.

b. 18 October 1961

Bobby McFerrin

b. 11 March 1950

A vocalist who performs entirely unaccompanied (unless you count a bottle of mineral water), McFerrin has not only great vocal agility but immense stamina. He can hold an audience entranced for an hour and a half with his sheer virtuosity. There are moments when, if you close your eyes, you could swear that there were two singers up there on stage, and possibly a drummer as well. To sing a melody in falsetto while sketching in a bass line two octaves below is a considerable feat, but to produce clicking and swishing sounds at the same time is officially impossible. But with him it doesn't look in the least like showing off. Everything has a clear musical function, and sometimes the effects are so lightly done that they pass almost unnoticed. The album on which he unveiled all this was entitled simply *The Voice*.

Stanley Jordan

b. 31 July 1959

The guitar comes in many shapes, but there is only one way to play it: you pluck the strings with one hand while the other one fingers the notes. At least, that was the case until Stanley Jordan came along. He devised a way of using both hands to do both jobs. The result sounds like two – sometimes three – guitars playing simultaneously.

Roughly speaking, what he does is this: he taps the strings instead of plucking them, treating the guitar fingerboard rather like the keys of a piano. Using a very sensitive electric guitar, he doesn't have to exert force on the strings to make them ring; the merest touch will bring forth a sound. The process is far more complicated than it sounds, and it comes as no surprise to learn that Jordan is a graduate of Princeton. His style is charming, perhaps a little over-elaborate at times, but with a natural, unforced swing.

THE BRITONS

Five of the best – *not the five best*

Humphrey Lyttelton
b. 23 May 1921

Although he formed his first band in 1948, and has been leading one ever since, Humph's position is far more important than that of a veteran bandleader. Trumpeter, composer, author, critic, broadcaster and wit – he is the figurehead of what might be called the Sensible Party in British jazz. He plays brisk and fiery trumpet in the post-Armstrong manner and his music has always been quite adventurous within the mainstream idiom. His three volumes of memoirs are hilarious and elegantly written and his weekly jazz record programme is so popular that when the BBC shortened it by ten minutes public protest made them put them back again.

Ronnie Scott
b. 28 January 1927

Because one of the world's most famous jazz clubs has his name on it, Ronnie Scott is often called a saxophone-playing club owner, when really he's a club-owning saxophone player. He was one of the founders of British modern jazz, travelling to New York as a ship's musician in the late forties, to hear Parker, Gillespie and company at first hand. Ever since then, it has been unwise to underrate Ronnie Scott as a jazz musician. In the fifties he co-led the Jazz Couriers, perhaps the best British jazz group ever, with the late Tubby Hayes. His current quintet is a superb little band which plays all over the world.

Sandy Brown
b. 25 February 1929
d. 15 March 1975

Almost certainly, Sandy Brown is the only jazz musician to record in a building which he had designed himself. A distinguished acoustic architect, he was also one of Britain's most original jazz musicians. His thick, vehement clarinet tone might have found favour in the trad boom, were it not for the wayward harmonic sophistication of his improvisations – and his detestation of the banjo. He was a wonderful blues player and composed dozens of idiosyncratic tunes, often with an African hi-life flavour. Sandy, who died in 1975, was also a very witty writer, and a collection of his work – 'The McJazz Manuscripts' – was published after his death. It was Sandy who coined the most delicate euphemism for 'drunk': he referred to it as 'being somewhat over-refreshed'.

Peter King
b. 11 August 1940

The finest alto saxophonist that Britain has ever produced, and one of the finest in the world today, Peter King should be an international celebrity. That he's not is partly the fault of his own modest nature and partly because British jazz fans have always tended to ignore what is under their noses. It is the twists and turns of his phrasing, especially his habit of topping an apparently complete statement with a series of elegant afterthoughts, that make Peter King such a delight to listen to, along with a passionate tone and phenomenal technique.

John Surman
b. 30 August 1944

John Surman is a genial West Countryman whose bemused, self-deprecating manner fails to conceal the fact that he is one of Europe's most accomplished and daring jazz musicians. On his main instrument, the baritone saxophone, he produces a rich and sonorous tone that has often been compared with that of the late Harry Carney, keystone of the Ellington orchestra. Whenever this is mentioned he cringes, scratches his thatched head and searches wildly for means of escape, but the comparison is just. In Surman's hands the unwieldy instrument moves with a kind of massive grace. Like many British musicians, John Surman is better appreciated abroad than at home. In recent years he has worked mainly on the Continent, where he is regarded as a jazz master.

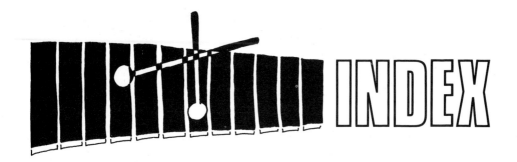

INDEX

Page numbers in *italic* indicate main references